W9-BAH-951

MAO ZEDONG'S

CHINA

KATHLYN GAY

TWENTY-FIRST CENTURY BOOKS   MINNEAPOLIS

Consultant: John Delury, Ph.D. in Chinese History, Yale University

Copyright © 2008 by Kathlyn Gay

All rights reserved. International copyright secured. No part of this book
may be reproduced, stored in a retrieval system, or transmitted in any form
or by any means—electronic, mechanical, photocopying, recording, or
otherwise—without prior written permission of Lerner Publishing Group,
Inc., except for the inclusion of brief quotations in an acknowledged review.

Twenty-First Century Books
A division of Lerner Publishing Group, Inc.
241 First Avenue North
Minneapolis, MN 55401 U.S.A.

Website address: www.lernerbooks.com

Library of Congress Cataloging-in-Publication Data

Gay, Kathlyn.
    Mao Zedong's China / by Kathlyn Gay.
        p.   cm. — (Dictatorships)
      ISBN 978–0–8225–7285–5 (lib. bdg. : alk. paper)
        1. China—History—1949–1976—Juvenile literature. 2. Mao, Zedong,
    1893–1976—Juvenile literature.   I. Title.
    DS777.55.G375 2008
    951.05092—dc22   2007005083

Manufactured in the United States of America
1 2 3 4 5 6 – DP – 13 12 11 10 09 08

CONTENTS

INTRODUCTION: "HAIL THE VICTORY" 6

CHAPTER 1: FROM DYNASTIES TO A REPUBLIC 10

CHAPTER 2: MAO'S RISE TO POWER 30

CHAPTER 3: CREATING THE PEOPLE'S REPUBLIC 48

CHAPTER 4: MILLIONS OF DEATHS 62

CHAPTER 5: LIFE UNDER MAO'S DICTATORSHIP 78

CHAPTER 6: POWER STRUGGLES AND DEATHS 96

CHAPTER 7: POST-MAO TURMOIL
AND JUDGMENTS 116

WHO'S WHO? 126

TIMELINE .132

GLOSSARY 134

SELECTED BIBLIOGRAPHY 136

SOURCE NOTES 143

FURTHER READING AND WEBSITES 153

INDEX 156

"HAIL

PEOPLE GATHERED ALONG SIDEWALKS on a January afternoon in 1949. They waited anxiously and with high expectations. At exactly 4:00 P.M., a parade of two hundred to three hundred soldiers of the People's Liberation Army marched six abreast into Beiping, as Beijing, China, was called at the time. A truck with loudspeakers accompanied the troops and repeated a message, "Welcome to the Liberation Army on its arrival in Beiping! Congratulations to the people of Beiping on their liberation!" Hundreds of students marched behind the soldiers, and trucks carrying more students, soldiers, and civilians followed.

An even larger victory parade took place three days later, with infantry, cavalry, tanks, heavy artillery, jeeps, and many other vehicles. Spectators applauded enthusiastically as thousands of students and workers marched. Some carried banners and pictures of the

THE VICTORY!"

THE PEOPLE OF BEIPING (BEIJING, CHINA) WELCOME CHINESE COMMUNIST forces entering the city in early 1949. Mao Zedong's portrait is raised in the center behind them.

leader of the Chinese Communist Party (CCP), Mao Zedong, also spelled Mao Tse-Tung. (In Chinese the family name appears before the given name, and the CCP leader usually was known simply by his family name Mao—or his CCP title, Chairman Mao.) The parades marked a major CCP victory in the Chinese Civil War (1927–1950) and the beginning of the People's Republic of China (PRC).

Mao and his delegates went to Tiananmen Square in the heart of the capital. The square is named for the huge Tiananmen, meaning, "gate of heavenly peace," at the northern end of this large public space. The huge gate is actually a vivid red building. It stands more than 143 feet (44 meters) high and almost 206 feet (63 m) wide. On the front of Tiananmen were two giant photographs—one of Mao and one of a prominent Red (Communist) Army general, Zhu De. Mao led delegates south of the gate, where they broke ground for a Monument to the People's Heroes.

Later in the year, a triumphant Mao declared in a speech that the Chinese people had been liberated from the Nationalist regime. "Hail the victory of the People's War of Liberation! Hail the founding of the People's Republic of China!" he cheered.

THE PEOPLE'S REPUBLIC

Mao returned to Tiananmen on October 1, 1949. He stood with members of his Communist government on the long rostrum, or platform, atop the gate. The country's new red flags with five gold stars flew. The single large star in the top corner stood for the Communist Party, and the four smaller stars represented the various social classes of Chinese people. Below in the square, thousands of citizens cheered as Mao proclaimed that the People's Republic of China had been established.

One of those citizens, Zhao Youping, was in Tiananmen Square that day. Decades later, she recalled, "We wore white shirts and blue trousers and carried red banners. The square looked so big, it was red everywhere: red flags, red lanterns. . . . We thought China was going

MAO DECLARED THE FOUNDING OF the People's Republic of China on October 1, 1949, in Tiananmen Square, Beiping, China.

to be a fair world forever," she told a reporter. Zhao, a committed Communist, had no idea that Mao would someday turn on the very people who had worked to bring about a "new China."

Over decades of revolution, war, and civil war, Mao pursued absolute control over China with political savvy and brutal suppression of his enemies. He established a totalitarian government that attempted to regulate virtually every aspect of society—the economy, politics, and shaping people's beliefs and attitudes. Mao organized peasants and workers, who were persuaded that he was acting on their behalf, and he depended on their unwavering support to reach his goals.

Mao's China, some historians say, came about because of his idealism and attempts to better the lives of the peasantry. Others argue that he was a ruthless dictator who, in his twenty-seven years of rule, was responsible for tens of millions of deaths.

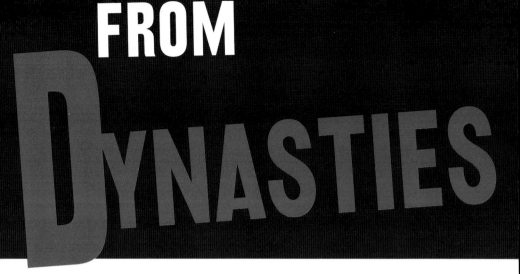

FROM DYNASTIES

FOR THOUSANDS OF YEARS BEFORE MAO BECAME CHINA'S head of state, the country was ruled by a succession of dynasties (families of rulers). Over generations, they passed their right to rule from one member to another.

The dynasty's territory was governed by a mixture of lords and local officials who were loyal to the emperor either through family ties, political patronage, or bureaucratic appointment. An emperor's armies fought numerous wars with tribes invading the kingdom or nomadic people attempting to control neighboring regions. When a dynasty was overthrown, another took its place until it also fell to the military might of more powerful rulers.

The last of the dynasties was called the Qing. Its rulers were not Chinese. Their original homeland was Manchuria, a region that in modern times is part of northeastern China. The Manchus had

REPUBLIC

MAO WAS BORN IN THIS THIRTEEN-ROOM MUD-BRICK FARMHOUSE IN THE village of Shaoshan, China, in 1893.

invaded China, capturing its capital in 1644 and controlling the country until 1911.

In the twilight of the Qing dynasty, Mao Zedong was born in the village of Shaoshan, near Changsha, the capital city of Hunan Province. He grew up during a time when the overthrow of the dynasty was imminent.

CHINESE PROVINCES

Hunan Province, where Mao was born, is located in southern China. It is one of the People's Republic of China's twenty-three provinces, which includes the disputed territory of Taiwan. Both Taiwan and the Beijing-based Communist government claim to be the government of all of China.

Chinese provinces are divisions similar to states in the United States. In addition to the provinces, China consists of five autonomous (self-ruled) minority regions, two special administrative regions (Hong Kong and Macao), and four cities that are directly under the administration of the central government.

OF PEASANT STOCK

Mao was born on December 26, 1893, to parents who were peasant farmers. Two younger brothers, Mao Zemin and Mao Zetan, were part of the family that included seven children, but only the three brothers survived childhood.

Like other peasants, the family incurred debts to survive. So Mao's father served in the army for years in order to pay off his loans. When he returned to Shaoshan, he was able to farm again.

At the age of six, Mao began to work on the farm, and after he entered the village primary school at the age of eight, he continued his farm tasks during the early morning and evening hours. By the time Mao was ten years old, his family owned 15 mu of land (which equaled 2.5 acres, or 1 hectare).

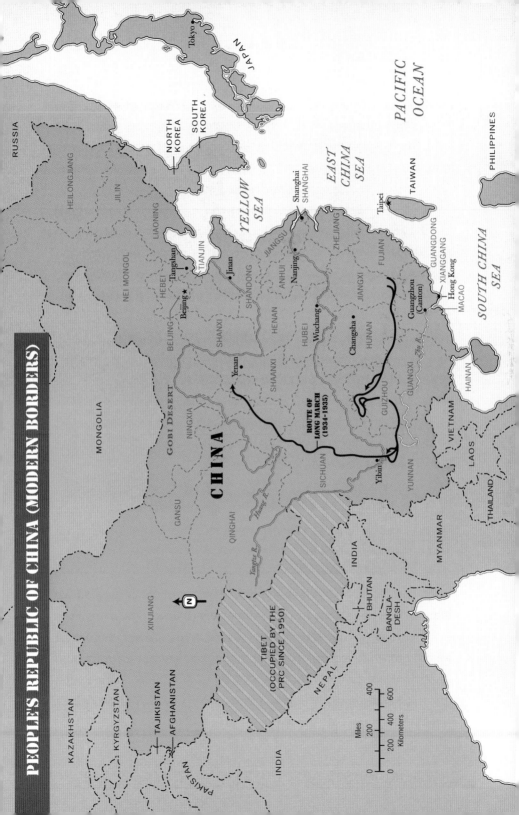

PEOPLE'S REPUBLIC OF CHINA (MODERN BORDERS)

ROUTE OF LONG MARCH (1934–1935)

TIBET (OCCUPIED BY THE PRC SINCE 1950)

CHINA

Miles
0   200   400
0   200   400   600
Kilometers

RUSSIA
MONGOLIA
KAZAKHSTAN
KYRGYZSTAN
TAJIKISTAN
AFGHANISTAN
PAKISTAN
XINJIANG
GOBI DESERT
NEI MONGOL
HEILONGJIANG
JILIN
LIAONING
NORTH KOREA
SOUTH KOREA
JAPAN
Tokyo
QINGHAI
GANSU
NINGXIA
SHAANXI
SHANXI
HEBEI
BEIJING
Beijing ★
Tangshan
TIANJIN
SHANDONG
Jinan
YELLOW SEA
HENAN
SICHUAN
Yenan
Yangtze R.
Huang R.
Yibin
GUIZHOU
YUNNAN
GUANGXI
HUBEI
Wuchang
HUNAN
Changsha
JIANGXI
ANHUI
JIANGSU
Nanjing
Shanghai
SHANGHAI
ZHEJIANG
FUJIAN
EAST CHINA SEA
Zhu R.
GUANGDONG
Guangzhou (Canton)
XIANGGANG
Hong Kong
MACAO
SOUTH CHINA SEA
HAINAN
TAIWAN
Taipei
PACIFIC OCEAN
PHILIPPINES
VIETNAM
LAOS
THAILAND
MYANMAR
BANGLA-DESH
BHUTAN
NEPAL
INDIA
N

They were able to raise enough rice to feed themselves and have a surplus, which Mao's father sold, enabling him to buy more land. The family eventually rose from being poor peasants to middle peasants to rich peasants. These distinctions would be used in later years to measure people's support for Mao's revolution.

In school Mao studied classic Confucian texts, which were used as the basis for examinations when applying for jobs in civil (public) service. Mao disliked the classics. He preferred reading novels and political tales of rebellions. Like other students, he would hide these stories inside his textbooks so his teacher would not discover them.

Mao had no love for his teacher and described him as "harsh and severe, frequently beating his students." When Mao was ten years old, he ran away from school, and years later, in an interview with British author Edgar Snow, he reported: "I was afraid to return home for fear of receiving a beating there, and set out in the general direction of the city. . . . I wandered for three days before I was found by my family." He discovered he had been traveling in circles and was only a few miles from his home.

REBELLIONS

Rebellions were common in the history of the Qing dynasty. While Mao was growing up, there were radical uprisings in various Chinese provinces. One occurred in 1900. Called the Boxer Rebellion, it was named for a secret society known as the Fists of Righteous Harmony—or Boxers, as Westerners dubbed them.

The Boxers were strongly opposed to the influence of foreign nations in China. By 1900 Austria, France, Germany, Great Britain,

Italy, Japan, and Russia had divided China into "spheres of influence." This meant that each nation claimed the exclusive privilege of trading in a specific Chinese region and refused to submit to the laws of the land. Because the Manchus had not been able to rid their country of such foreign influences, the Boxers also opposed the ruler then in power: Tzu Hsi, the empress dowager. (As the mother of the child emperor, she was given the title empress dowager.) The Boxers demanded that the Manchus and foreigners be driven from China.

The empress dowager, however, secretly aligned herself with the Boxers, who vented their fury on foreigners by attacking Christian missionaries and Chinese converts to Christianity. When the Boxers stormed the capital, the empress dowager and her court

A CHINESE BOXER *(LEFT)* HOLDS A FLAG AND WEAPONS IN 1900. BOXERS were opposed to foreign rule, including that of the Manchu empress dowager Tzu Hsi *(right)*.

did nothing to stop them. Foreign diplomats tried to defend themselves against twenty thousand Boxers who "advanced in a solid mass and carried standards of red and white cloth," according to one eyewitness. "Their yells were deafening, while the roar of gongs, drums and horns sounded like thunder."

An international relief force finally came to the aid of the diplomats and their families. The improvised army occupied the capital, forcing the empress dowager to disguise herself as a peasant to escape the city. In 1901 the fighting ended, and a peace treaty called the Boxer Protocol allowed foreign troops to be stationed in the capital and to patrol Chinese ports. The agreement outlawed the import of arms and ammunition. In addition, the treaty required that China pay back foreign nations for the losses they had suffered. The total amount was 450 million taels (weight measures) of silver—a huge amount of money at the time.

REVOLUTIONARY ACTIVITIES

Because of the humiliation of the Boxer Rebellion and other weaknesses of the imperial government, many Chinese began talking about and organizing for an outright revolution against the Qing. One prominent backer of revolution was Sun Yat-sen (1866–1925), who had been educated in the West. Sun advocated three basic principles: nationalism, democracy, and Socialism. These became known as the Three People's Principles. The nation, he declared, should be governed by Chinese, not foreign imperialists. Government leaders should be democratically elected. And wealth and land ownership should be equalized through a Socialist

WHAT IS SOCIALISM?

Socialism is an economic theory and a political system in which the government owns most of a nation's property and businesses. There are numerous variations of Socialism. Basically, however, in a Socialist society, the government or the community as a whole owns much of the nation's property and controls and operates many businesses and services. Under the more extreme forms of Socialism, people work and live cooperatively. All things are held or used in common. There is no private ownership of property or businesses.

system. By the time Mao was seventeen years of age, he was familiar with Sun's ideas.

Mao left the family farm when he was sixteen, after several years of a marriage that had been arranged when he was fourteen by his father—a common practice in China. Mao's wife died at the age of twenty-one, and later Mao declared that he had "never lived with her" and "did not consider her my wife."

Mao obtained most of his education in schools outside Shaoshan and was especially influenced by his schooling in 1911 at Changsha, the provincial capital. In Changsha he read numerous radical newspapers and "whatever he could find on Sun Yat-sen," according to historian Jonathan Spence.

While in Changsha, Mao and his classmates learned about a student uprising in Szechwan Province and a rebellion in the city of Wuchang in Hubei Province. Rebels seized Wuchang on October 10, 1911. This day became known as Double Ten (tenth day of the tenth month) National Day because it sparked the beginning of the

MAO *(FOURTH FROM LEFT)* **AND HIS CLASSMATES AT CHANGSHA IN 1911. MAO**
spent much of his time reading newspapers while in school in the provincial capital.

end for the Qing dynasty. Soon after the seizure of Wuchang, fifteen
provinces, one by one, seceded (broke away) from the empire and
openly rebelled against the Qing.

Mao and his friends also listened to a revolutionary speaker
who came to the Changsha classroom to denounce the Manchus.
"Four or five days after hearing this speech, I determined to join the
revolutionary army," Mao reported. He served for six months but
never engaged in combat. He was stationed at the Changsha garrison (military post). There he gained respect among the troops
because he was more educated than they were and sometimes
wrote letters for them. That led to some conceitedness on Mao's
part. As he noted, "Soldiers had to carry water in from outside the
city, but I, being a student, could not condescend to carrying, and
bought it from water peddlers."

While in the army, Mao continued his avid reading. He was excited about Socialist ideas and tried to share his enthusiasm in letters to classmates and friends. But "only one of them responded in agreement."

FORMING GOVERNMENTS AND POLITICAL PARTIES

After his military service, eighteen-year-old Mao enrolled in a variety of schools for short periods. Eventually he decided to teach himself by constantly reading and studying in the Hunan Provincial Library.

By this time, the revolution was over. The revolutionary forces had defeated the Qing dynasty quickly and a new republican government was set up in 1912. But there was a conflict between Sun Yat-sen and another leader, Yuan Shikai. Sun had established a provisional (temporary) republic that was based on his Three Principles idea. With his power base in Nanjing on the Yangtze River, Sun was proclaimed leader of the new government by his supporters. Yuan, a strong military leader, dominated northern China, and wanted to be the head of a government established in Beijing. To avoid a civil war, Sun agreed to allow Yuan to head the government, with Beijing as the capital.

A new political party, the Kuomintang had formed in the summer of 1912. Usually called the KMT, or the Nationalist Party, it was a merger of several smaller groups, one of which was founded by Sun Yat-sen. When an election for members of parliament (the lawmaking body of the republic) was held in 1913, Nationalists opposed Yuan and won a majority in the legislature.

Yuan retaliated by ordering the assassination of the Nationalist leader. He also dissolved the KMT and removed members of the party from parliament. Then he did away with parliament altogether and appointed a council made up of his followers. The council created a new constitution that made Yuan president for life. Yet Yuan had further plans for power—he wanted to establish a new dynasty with himself as emperor.

In late 1915 and early 1916, numerous southern provinces rebelled against Yuan. But the revolt was quickly crushed. Because Sun was one of the leaders of the rebellion, he and other instigators had to flee the country. Sun escaped to Japan, which had long been a safe haven for exiled Chinese reformers and intellectuals.

SUN YAT-SEN *(LEFT)* **AND YUAN SHIKAI** *(RIGHT)* **STRUGGLED FOR POWER** in China during the early part of the twentieth century.

Yuan died in June 1916. Warlords—military commanders ruling a territory—fought for control of the national government. These militarists supported their armies by taxing peasants and businesspeople. A decade of chaos followed as central and local governments crumbled and no leader emerged to unite the Chinese people.

WORLD WAR I

While political and military maneuverings were going on in China, World War I (1914–1918) was under way in Europe. Japan, as it frequently had done in the past, was threatening China. During Europe's "Great War," the Japanese joined the Allies (France, Russia, Britain, Italy, the United States, and others) against the Central powers that included Germany, Austro-Hungary, Bulgaria, and Turkey. There was little criticism from the Allies when Japan seized German settlements and naval bases in Shandong Province. The Japanese also took control of a railroad line that the Germans had built as well as coal mines along the railroad.

In 1915 the Japanese declared they would wage war against China if certain demands were not met. These Twenty-One Demands, as they were called, included Japanese control over Manchuria, parts of Mongolia, and the seized railroads and territory in Shandong. In the agreement, the Chinese were not allowed "to cede or lease to a third Power any harbour or bay or island along the coast of China" and were required to consult Japan whenever the government needed "the service of political, financial, or military advisers or instructors." In short, all the demands, if met, would have made China little more than a Japanese colony.

The Chinese parliament did not consent to the agreement, and Japan continued its war threats. But Yuan Shikai, who headed the Chinese government, communicated secretly with the Japanese, and he agreed to most of Japan's demands. A year after Yuan's death in 1917, the Chinese agreed to aid the European Allies who had supported the return of German territory to China. With that pledge, China sent 180,000 laborers to work behind Allied lines in Europe, digging trenches, repairing railroad lines and bridges, and providing other nonmilitary help. The Chinese labor allowed the Allied troops to keep up the fight to defeat the Germans.

After Germany's surrender in late 1918, China expected to win some concessions at the peace conference in Paris, France. China requested that Japan's Twenty-One Demands be withdrawn, but conference participants—who represented the United States, Great Britain, France, and Italy—said they had no authority to deal with

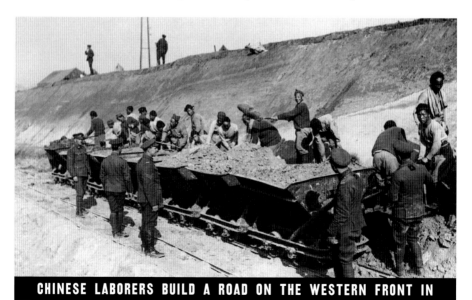

CHINESE LABORERS BUILD A ROAD ON THE WESTERN FRONT IN Europe during World War I. The Chinese helped the European Allies by filling nonmilitary positions.

the agreement. U.S. president Woodrow Wilson previously had expressed strong support for China on the Shandong issue.

But in the end, Wilson did not insist on a resolution. He was more concerned about establishing the League of Nations. Wilson believed such an international organization would prevent war through peaceful negotiations. He went along with the Allied powers in order to get their support for the League of Nations Covenant, which was included in a treaty with Germany signed at the Palace of Versailles in France. However, the United States did not join the league and did not ratify the Versailles Peace Treaty because of opposition by the U.S. Senate. The disappointed Chinese also refused to sign the treaty, and Japan remained dominant over China.

When Chinese students learned about their government's secret arrangements and the decisions made at the Paris peace conference, they "were greatly shocked," as one university student put it. "We at once awoke to the fact that foreign nations were still selfish and materialistic and that they were all great liars."

Protests spread from university students to merchants and workers across the nation. It was the first time in modern Chinese history that the masses had risen up in an outburst of nationalism. Some historians have called it a turning point, the beginning of a new political and cultural period.

THE MAY FOURTH MOVEMENT

One of the main protest events occurred on May 4, 1919. Students at Peking National University marked the anniversary of Japan's Twenty-One Demands by holding a "National Shame Day." They protested foreigners in their country and the warlords who had accommodated them. People boycotted (refused to buy) Japanese products. The agitation became known as the May Fourth Movement, and it continued throughout the month. Police arrested hundreds of people, most of them students, but public pressure brought about their release.

Mao Zedong was in Changsha at the time of the May Fourth Movement. He had been studying in Peking but returned home to see his ill mother and to find a job. He had graduated from a teacher training institution, and a Changsha school hired him as a history teacher. He also began editing and writing for a student journal. His articles in July and August 1919 presented his emerging political views. In his manifesto (declaration of views), he pointed out that a revolution in Russia in 1917 had "overthrown the

THE RUSSIAN REVOLUTION

In 1917 Russia experienced great turmoil. In March a revolution erupted and the czar (emperor) was overthrown. A provisional government was formed, while at the same time, radical revolutionaries set up soviets—councils of workers and soldiers. The soviets created their own form of government, and the provisional government steadily lost control.

Among the revolutionaries was Vladimir Ilyitch Lenin (1870–1924), the leader of the Bolshevik Party. Late in 1917, Lenin and the Bolsheviks seized control of the Russian government.

aristocrats and driven out the rich." He argued that the same thing could happen in China:

> The world is ours, the nation is ours, society is ours. If we do not speak, who will speak? If we do not act, who will act? If we do not rise up and fight, who will rise up and fight? . . . We must act energetically to carry out the great union of the popular masses. . . . Our golden age, our age of brightness and splendour lies ahead!

Two other articles, which were excerpts from Mao's manifesto, appeared in subsequent issues of the student journal. He cited the Russian example of social reforms that other countries had undertaken and urged people to "arise and imitate them."

Lenin and his followers were devoted Marxists. Like the German philosopher Karl Marx (1818–1883), Lenin believed that private property should be abolished and a classless society established through revolutionary means. He also believed that these goals should be met no matter the cost in human life.

After taking power, Lenin renamed the Bolsheviks, calling them the Communist Party. He called for all property to be taken over by the government and for all land to be redistributed among the peasants. Lenin became head of the government, but chaos and civil war raged for years. He did not establish full control until 1921. Then in 1922, the Russian empire became the Union of Soviet Socialist Republics (USSR).

BECOMING A MARXIST

The ruling Chinese militarist in Hunan Province, General Zhang Jingyao, shut down Mao's journal before the fifth issue could be printed. Yet Mao continued to write for other publications. He also organized student groups to strike in protest of Zhang's attacks on the province's educational system and against his brutal troops and corrupt government.

Zhang ruthlessly subdued the strike, and Mao and others who politically opposed Zhang were in a dangerous position. Mao decided to go to Beijing once more and then on to Shanghai in an effort to gain support for overthrowing Zhang. In Mao's view, "only mass political power, secured through mass action, could guarantee the realization of dynamic reforms."

While in Beijing, Mao met with the family of Yang Changji. Yang had been one of Mao's teachers and mentors at the Changsha Normal School. He later became a professor of history at Peking University and had befriended Mao when Mao was in the city. Yang was very ill and died a few weeks after Mao arrived. Mao stayed on to comfort Yang's wife and his daughter, Yang Kaihui.

Mao became romantically involved with Yang Kaihui, an active Communist, and he was greatly influenced by their discussions on Communism and the books he read on the subject. "By the summer of 1920 I had become, in theory and to some extent in action, a Marxist, and from this time on I considered myself a Marxist," he said.

As a Marxist, Mao (like Lenin) believed in the theories of Marx and his fellow philosopher Friedrich Engels (1820–1895). Marx and Engels published their ideas in *The Communist Manifesto* (1848), one of the books Mao had read. It included a description of what the

KARL MARX *(LEFT)* **AND FRIEDRICH ENGELS** *(RIGHT)* **EXPLAINED THEIR** Communist theories in the *The Communist Manifesto*, published in 1848.

philosophers called scientific Socialism—theories based on a scientific study of history.

Marx argued that throughout history, people have been divided into classes and that class struggles are born of economics. People who control the land and means of production accumulate wealth and power, while the proletariat (working class) is powerless. Marx predicted that the proletariat would rise up against the ruling class in a revolution, which is what happened in Russia.

ORGANIZING THE CCP

Although the majority of Chinese had little knowledge or experience with Communism, a fledgling Chinese Communist Party

A SMALL BEGINNING

Historians have given different accounts of the CCP's First Congress, or meeting. For example, China historian Jonathan Spence wrote that at the First Congress, fifteen delegates represented "fifty-three Chinese Communists who were then affiliated with the Party in one form or another."

Jacques Guillermaz, a historian who studied the Chinese Communist Party, declared that seven regional groups organized with a total of fifty-seven members. Twelve delegates represented them at the First National Congress of the CCP.

And Mao expert Stuart Schram noted: "Among those attending [the First Congress] were two delegates from each of the six groups" of Chinese Communists in existence in 1921, "plus one representative of the Chinese in Japan, thirteen in all."

(CCP) was formed in 1921. The organization received advice and funding from the Soviet Union and agents of the Communist International (or Comintern for short), an international organization designed to spread Soviet Communism and foster revolution.

Mao Zedong attended the CCP's First Congress representing Hunan Province but apparently did not play a significant role. He was told, however, to go back to Hunan and organize party members. He became provincial secretary of the CCP and, in that capacity, took part in a "vigorous labor movement." He reported that the Communist Party "organized twenty trade unions among miners, railway workers, municipal employees, printers, and workers in the government mint . . . [but] very little was done among the peasants." Mao emphasized that the CCP should have paid more attention to the farmers, who were the largest segment of China's population.

During this time, Mao and Yang Kaihui were living together and since late 1920 had considered themselves married. They had their first child, a boy, in 1922. Another son was born the following year.

AN ALLIANCE

By 1922 the CCP had grown somewhat but was still a small, weak organization. It had few means to reach the masses with Communist ideas. At the urging of the Comintern, the Chinese Communists formed an alliance with Sun Yat-sen's Nationalist Party, or Kuomintang. The purpose was to rid the country of militarists controlling much of China and to unify the nation under a Soviet-type Communism. The Soviets instructed CCP members to cooperate with the KMT.

Sun sent his military aide, Chiang Kai-shek, to Moscow to study the Soviet military and political systems. When Chiang returned to China, he established the Whampoa Military Academy in Guangzhou (now Canton), where Sun's government had its headquarters. Chiang became generalissimo, or commander in chief, of the Nationalist forces.

Sun Yat-sen died in 1925, and the following year, Chiang led the combined KMT and CCP troops in a successful military campaign against China's warlords. Mao was then in Hunan Province and was witness to the victory of the "United Front" forces over Hunan's military rulers. At the time, some had hoped that the KMT and the CCP would hold together. But events were to prove otherwise.

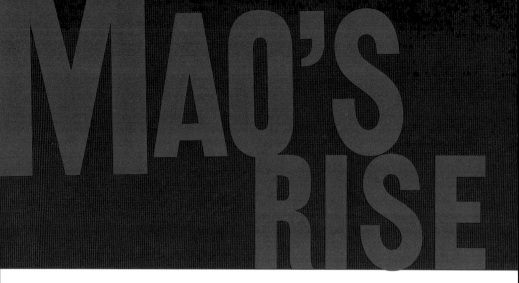

MAO'S RISE

AFTER THE ALLIANCE BETWEEN THE CCP AND THE KMT IN 1922, Mao Zedong's political activities became increasingly hectic. In Shanghai he was elected to the CCP's Central Executive Committee. He also became a member of the Executive Committee of the KMT. His duties included coordinating revolutionary efforts of the KMT and the CCP, developing propaganda materials, and reporting on efforts of peasants to join the revolution.

But there was growing tension in the KMT. Two rival factions (groups) competed for dominance: the right wing and left wing. Those on the right were led by Chiang. They wanted to cooperate with merchants and military leaders, strengthen the nation, and destroy leftist challenges. Those on the left leaned toward Communists and their support of workers and peasants in the revolution.

THE PEASANT MOVEMENT

By 1925 a peasant movement was well under way. Poor peasants had organized associations and cooperatives in various provinces. Their goal was to liberate themselves from harsh conditions that the gentry (rich landowners) forced upon them, such as high rents for farmland, payable in half or more of the harvests. Landlords were likely to beat peasants for nonpayment of rents or just to humiliate them.

Hundreds of thousands of peasants rose up in revolt against wealthy landlords. Peasant associations became the authorities in villages. They seized landowners' property, took their livestock and crops, executed some, or forced them to flee to cities.

THE FIVE STAGES OF HISTORY

Marxists, such as Mao, believed that all societies progressed through five stages of history—primitive Communism, slavery, feudalism, capitalism, and advanced Communism. They labeled prehistoric societies as primitive Communists. People during this period lived simple lives in small communities. The good of the group was of far more importance than that of the individual.

Slave societies were based upon the labor of slaves for the good of their owners. Feudalism is the term given to the system of obligations between rulers, landowners, and common folk as practiced in dynastic China and Europe in the Middle Ages. Basically, under the dynastic Chinese system, an emperor appointed lords who were loyal to him. The lords had power over the common folks and peasants, extracting taxes and services from them to benefit the emperor's kingdom. (In recent years, historians have begun to question exactly how strict feudal ties really were, however.) Capitalism is the system in use in the United States and many Western nations. Most businesses and industries are in the hands of private owners. Advanced Communism is the classless society predicted by Marx.

The Five-Stage Theory was developed to describe European history. But in the twentieth century, Chinese Marxists started applying it to their own past. They considered rural China to be "stuck" in the feudal stage, when landlords exploited landless peasants. Chinese Marxists promised their revolution would allow China to "leap" into the final stage of advanced Communism.

As Mao put it in a report, "The broad peasant masses have risen to fulfill their historic mission . . . to overthrow the rural feudal power."

At the same time, warlords or coalitions of warlords in the provinces were brutalizing people, and Chiang sent the United Forces armies to battle the militarists. In the 1926 Northern Expedition, peasants provided aid, such as food, shelter, and scouts for the troops, and the expedition successfully removed many warlords from power. Yet KMT-CCP leaders did not see much potential for peasant revolutionary activities, even though Mao repeatedly tried to emphasize their importance.

Mao was appointed director of the CCP-KMT Peasant Commission, and he spent more than a month in Hunan Province investigating peasant activities. In a lengthy report written in 1927, he emphasized that the peasant movement would greatly benefit the national revolution. Mao declared that "several hundred million peasants will rise like a mighty storm. . . . They will send all imperialists, warlords, corrupt officials, local tyrants and evil gentry into their graves."

Mao acknowledged that many people thought the peasants were too violent and had gone too far in punishing those who had been their persecutors. But he countered with what became oft-quoted words:

. . . a revolution is not the same as inviting people to dinner, or writing an essay, or painting a picture, or doing fancy needlework. . . . A revolution is an uprising, an act of violence by which one class overthrows another.

Some Communists rejected Mao's view because it was not in line with the strict Marxist theory that urban industrial workers should lead the revolution. In addition, the Communists did not want to risk alienating the right wing of the KMT who feared that a peasant uprising would threaten unification of China.

A CCP-KMT SPLIT

In 1927 Chiang Kai-shek seized on the opportunity to turn on the Communists in the KMT. He believed their activities and growing power were obstructing efforts to unite China under one Nationalist government. He also feared that his influence was fading, and he was determined to remain in control. Chiang expelled Communists from the KMT, and in a bloody confrontation, his KMT forces attacked workers in Shanghai and other cities. Thousands of Communists were captured and executed, and terrorist groups shot anyone suspected of sympathizing with the Communists. The massacres sparked the beginning of a civil war between Nationalists and Communists.

Mao, who had set up peasant soviets in Hunan Province, escaped the KMT purge. He fled to a remote mountain region in southeastern China. In the mountainous Jinggangshan area, the government had little, if any, control. There were no roads, and people traveled by foot or on horses or mules along narrow mountain paths. It was a relatively safe place to set up a Communist stronghold. There Mao and a military commander Zhu De (1886–1976) organized peasants, bandits, and rebellious KMT soldiers into a guerrilla fighting force known as the Red Army.

The Red Army carried a flag with a red background and a white star with a hammer and sickle in its center. The color red was associated with revolutionary Socialism and also with the Communists, or "Reds," who fought in the Russian civil war (1917–1920).

RULES FOR RED ARMY SOLDIERS

During the Red Army's time in the mountains, Mao set down explicit rules for his soldiers. Many soldiers had little experience with organized warfare. The soldiers needed to obey authority to be effective, and Mao created simple rules that the soldiers learned to follow.

Called the Three Rules of Discipline, they were (1) obey orders; (2) don't take anything from the workers and peasants; and (3) turn in all things taken from local bullies and landlords. Along with establishing these rules, Mao introduced political training in the army. As he put it:

> [T]he Red Army exists not merely to fight; besides fighting to destroy the enemy's military strength, it should also shoulder such important tasks as agitating the masses, organizing them, arming them, and helping them set up revolutionary political power, and even establishing organizations of the Communist Party.

Later, Mao added Eight Points for Attention:
1. Speak politely.
2. Pay fairly for what you buy.
3. Return everything you borrow.
4. Pay for anything you damage.
5. Don't hit or swear at people.
6. Don't damage crops.
7. Don't take liberties with women.
8. Don't ill-treat captives.

All of these rules were reissued in 1947 to guide the People's Liberation Army (The Red Army had been renamed the People's Liberation Army, or PLA, in 1946). The relatively disciplined behavior of the CCP forces was an important factor in the ultimate victory of the Communists over the KMT.

China's Red Army prepared to fight the local militias, who were paid by landlords to prevent peasant uprisings. They also fought the KMT's White Army, as Mao called it. Mao used the terms *White Army* and *White regime* frequently to indicate the forces that opposed the Reds in China as well as in Russia.

FIGHTING THE ENEMY

Because the Red Army was so much weaker than the KMT troops, Mao planned extended warfare using mobile and guerrilla tactics. Small units moved around to various positions and staged surprise attacks on the larger enemy. Mao summarized the strategy in the slogans: "When the enemy advances, we retreat! When the enemy halts and encamps, we trouble them! When the enemy seeks to avoid a battle, we attack! When the enemy retreats, we pursue!"

The Red Army was small and ill equipped. The men had few heavy clothes to ward off the cold. Some were malnourished, and hundreds were wounded in the many skirmishes they fought. In spite of poor conditions, the Reds often gained recruits by helping the peasants. Captured KMT troops also joined the Reds. Mao explained that recruitment was possible because of equality within the Red Army ranks, the freedom to speak out, the informality of daily routine, and the fact that the troops had "a little sum for pocket money." This, Mao reported,

[G]ives great satisfaction to the soldiers. The newly captured soldiers in particular feel that our army and the Kuomintang army are worlds apart. They feel that, though in material life they are worse off in the Red Army than in the White Army, spiritually they are liberated.

While Mao was in the mountain region, his wife and children were in Changsha. Mao was unable to contact them since there was a price on his head—huge rewards were offered for killing or capturing him. And Yang Kaihui had no way to leave Changsha and join Mao in the mountains. In 1930 she was captured by the KMT and executed.

Meanwhile, Mao had a new partner, He Zizhen, a feisty young Communist who was a member of the bandit forces in the mountains. She and Mao became lovers and eventually married and had five children.

A BASE IN JIANGXI PROVINCE

In 1929 Mao left the mountainous Jinggangshan area for another mountainous area, closer to the Fujian Province, a place that came to be known as the Jiangxi Soviet. There he was able to gain recruits and needed supplies. The Red Army began winning territory, and between 1930 and 1934, the KMT tried repeatedly to stop Mao Zedong and his troops.

When the KMT launched campaigns with hundreds of thousands of soldiers to destroy the Communists, the much smaller Red Army was able to erode, frustrate, and beat back the Nationalists. The Reds waited for KMT troops to penetrate their territory. Then, using guerrilla tactics, various bands of men moved about constantly to ambush one KMT regiment after another.

In the fall of 1933, however, the KMT surrounded the Communists' strongholds. Against Mao's advice, the Communists used new strategies. They launched full-frontal attacks on the KMT, "abandoning our former tactics of maneuver," Mao reported. The Red Army could not overcome the far superior KMT forces because it "was neither technically nor spiritually at its best."

After holding off the KMT for a year, the Communists were forced to retreat in October 1934. They began a 6,000-mile (9,656-kilometer) march, fighting along the way from Jiangxi Province in the south to Shaanxi Province in the north, where they would set up Communist headquarters.

MAO ZEDONG RIDES HIS WHITE HORSE ON THE LONG MARCH FROM southern China to northern China in 1934–1935. Mao's leadership during the 6,000-mile (9,656 km) ordeal helped solidify his place at the top of the CCP.

THE LONG MARCH

Much has been written about the Long March, and diverse statistics and facts have been compiled about this yearlong trek. For example:

- Somewhere between 100,000 and 200,000 troops began the march.
- Thousands of Red Army soldiers were left behind because of injuries. Many were killed by the KMT.
- Red Army troops traveled over eighteen mountain ranges, through swamps, and across twenty-four rivers to reach their destination.
- One of the ranges that the soldiers crossed was the Great Snow Mountain, where the terrain was always snow covered and glaciers created treacherous chasms.
- The limbs of some soldiers froze and had to be amputated.
- Food was scarce, and soldiers went without eating for days.
- Because of bouts with malaria, Mao did not accompany the troops on foot but rode on horseback or sometimes was carried on a litter (a stretcher).
- Only a few women accompanied the soldiers on the trek. He Zizhen, who was pregnant at the time, went along with Mao, but they left their two-year-old son behind with Mao's brother. (The boy disappeared after the brother left for combat.)
- Tens of thousands of soldiers died on the march, and only 7,000 to 8,000 Red Army troops survived.

After the Red Army reached Shaanxi Province in October 1935, Mao established a Communist base in Yenan. There Mao and He set up living quarters in a cave house, a type of dwelling that had been common for centuries in this border region of China. The caves were built into hillsides, and a door set into a wooden frame covered the opening. Although primitive, caves were "good protection from the extremes of heat and cold that afflicted this arid region."

It was in Yenan at the cave house that Edgar Snow interviewed Mao in 1936. Snow's published report about his visit enhanced Mao's image in Europe and encouraged other Westerners to travel to northwest China. Mao also gained respect when he spoke out against Japan's increasing aggression toward China. Five years earlier, in 1931, Japanese forces had invaded and seized Manchuria, which was rich in the raw materials Japan needed for industrial development. Mao advocated an end to the civil war and a united front against the Japanese.

Mao declared that in an anti-Japanese war, all members of the Communist Party should be prepared to fight as well as to organize and take part in mass movements. In his view, "Every Communist must grasp the truth: 'Political power grows out of the barrel of a gun.'" He pointed out "we do not desire war; but war can only be abolished through war—in order to get rid of the gun, we must first grasp it in our hand."

In late 1936, Chiang also went to Shaanxi. The KMT leader hoped to work out a plan with Zhang Xueliang, a warlord and former ruler of Manchuria, to destroy Mao and the Communists. The "Young Marshall," as Zhang was called, had a sizable army that had been fighting the Reds, and his troops remained with him when the Japanese forced Zhang out of Manchuria.

However, Zhang had become increasingly frustrated with Chiang, who was more interested in eliminating the Communists than in stopping Japanese invaders. So during Chiang's visit, Marshall Zhang had his men kidnapped the Nationalist leader and held him until he agreed to unite with the Communists in a war against Japan.

A SHAKY ALLIANCE

Some progress was made toward unity in early 1937. The CCP Central Committee offered to end its efforts to overthrow the Nationalist government, to eliminate its own government, and to create a special regional administration in Shaanxi as part of the Republic of China. The CCP also would allow the Nationalist government to direct the Red Army, would stop confiscating land, and would apply democratic principles and hold elections.

In exchange, the Communists asked the KMT to end the civil war, to release all political prisoners, to prepare immediately for resistance against the Japanese, to improve the people's standard of living, and to hold a national congress regarding methods to ensure salvation of the country. The KMT responded with its own proposal that included making the Red Army a part of the Nationalist forces and stopping Communist propaganda and the class struggle.

Although these propositions were not accepted in their entirety, the two sides agreed in September 1937 to create a second "united front" to fight the Japanese. For a time, Mao and his army, renamed the Eighth Route Army (part of the National Revolutionary Army), and Chiang's KMT forces cooperated.

But there was growing tension between the KMT and the Communists. The Communists expanded their operations in the villages of North China and increased their troops. Chiang saw this as a threat to his dominance and his ability to deal with the Japanese once they were forced out of China.

JAPANESE AGGRESSION

For years Japan had made aggressive attempts to control portions of China. Since the invasion of Manchuria in 1931, Japan had steadily encroached on northern China while looking for aid from Europeans who would support them against the Soviet Union.

The Japanese were convinced that the Soviets would prevent them from achieving their goal of an Asian empire. Nazi Germany agreed to a pact with Japan in November 1936. Italy joined the pact a year later. This Anti-Comintern Pact supposedly was designed to prevent Communism from spreading worldwide. It also included a secret procedure to protect the pact countries from a Soviet attack. In addition, Germany recognized the Manchurian government that had been set up by Japan.

Tensions increased in late June 1937. Japanese troops were practicing military maneuvers near the Lugou Bridge (also known as the Marco Polo Bridge). The Japanese demanded that they be allowed to search for a missing soldier in an area south of Peking. Chinese troops did not comply, and on July 6, a shooting confrontation began that sparked eight years of war between Japan and China.

In late 1937, Japanese forces seized control of the Nationalist capital of Peking. Chiang moved the capital to Nanjing (Nanking).

MARCO POLO BRIDGE

The Italian explorer Marco Polo (1254–1324) described the Lugou Bridge in his book *The Travels of Marco Polo*. Thus the structure is sometimes referred to as the Marco Polo Bridge. It is southwest of Peking and crosses the Yongding River.

The original bridge was built in 1192, but parts of it were washed away and had to be rebuilt. It is constructed of stone blocks. Decorating the railings are 485 stone lions, each in a different position. At each end of the bridge, which is 874 feet (266 m) in length, carved elephants and lions stand guard. Numerous Internet sites include photographs of the bridge along with factual information about it.

MEMBERS OF THE CHINESE ARMY DEFEND A SANDBAG BARRICADE ON THE Marco Polo Bridge in July 1937.

After the Japanese captured Shanghai on the east coast, they advanced toward Nanjing. In early December 1937, Japanese troops attacked the city and over the next six weeks committed atrocities that some have called the most brutal in world history. In what is known as the Rape of Nanjing, an estimated three hundred thousand Chinese were killed—gassed, bayoneted, burned alive, machine-gunned, or mutilated until dead. About twenty thousand women, girls, and elderly nuns were raped and then killed.

IN THIS CHILLING EXAMPLE OF BRUTALITY, JAPANESE TROOPS PRACTICE
their bayoneting skills on live Chinese prisoners in Nanjing in December 1937.

CAPITAL NAME CHANGES

Beijing, modern China's capital, has gone through numerous name changes. From 1928 to 1937, it was called Beiping, which meant "northern peace." The Kuomintang/Nationalist government in Nanjing, meaning "southern capital," changed the name from Beijing (northern capital) to Beiping to underscore that it was not the nation's capital. When the Japanese occupied the city in 1937, they established a puppet (Japanese-controlled) government, which named the city Beijing again. After Japan's defeat in 1945, the city reverted to Beiping. Finally, when the Communist Party took power in 1949, it made Beijing the capital of the nation and restored its name.

An eyewitness account by a *New York Times* reporter, Frank Tillman Durdin, was published on December 18, 1937. He reported widespread deaths of civilians, with "dead on every street" and looting of almost all buildings throughout the city. The report also described mass executions of Chinese soldiers and those in civilian clothes suspected of being in the military.

END OF THE ALLIANCE

By 1941 collaboration between the KMT and CCP was falling apart. Meanwhile, World War II (1939–1945) was being waged in Europe.

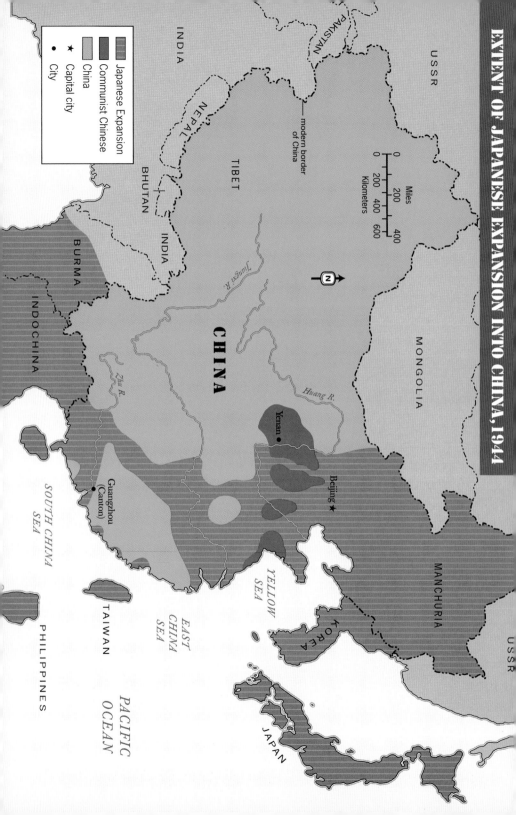

Japanese Expansion
Communist Chinese
China
★ Capital city
● City

USSR

PAKISTAN

INDIA

NEPAL

BHUTAN

INDIA

TIBET

modern border
of China

CHINA

BURMA

INDOCHINA

Zhu R.

Jangzi R.

Huang R.

Yenan ●

Beijing ★

MONGOLIA

MANCHURIA

KOREA

USSR

N

0   200   400   600
Kilometers

0   200   400
Miles

SOUTH CHINA SEA

Guangzhou
(Canton) ●

TAIWAN

YELLOW SEA

EAST CHINA SEA

PACIFIC OCEAN

JAPAN

PHILIPPINES

Then on December 7, 1941, Japan bombed the U.S. naval base at Pearl Harbor in the Hawaiian Islands. This act catapulted the United States into the war. As the Japanese sent their forces to fight Americans in the Pacific, their strength to battle the Chinese diminished. But the Chinese-Japanese war continued.

The United States sent aid to the Chinese and built an airbase so U.S. planes could launch bombing attacks on Japan. During this time, the only unifying factor for the CCP and the KMT was the struggle against Japan. When the Japanese surrendered in 1945, civil strife in China intensified.

During the next few years, the Communists, with their guerrilla tactics and peasant support, were in a better position to gain territory and power than the KMT. By January 1949, the Communists were able to gain control of the capital, and it was renamed Beijing. Between April and November, they took over other major cities. The KMT was forced to flee to Taiwan. There Chiang set up a Nationalist government and became a dictatorial ruler, stifling any opposition.

While the Nationalists were losing control, Mao held a series of meetings with delegates to the Chinese People's Political Consultative Conference. At one gathering on September 21, 1949, he declared in his opening address that the conference was "representative of the people of the whole country and enjoys their trust and support." Mao told more than six hundred delegates that their "work will go down in the history of mankind, demonstrating that the Chinese people, comprising one quarter of humanity, have now stood up."

It was a declaration that the People's Republic of China had been established. Mao Zedong publicly announced the formation of the "new China" on October 1, 1949, in Tiananmen Square.

CHAPTER 3

CREATING

AFTER MAO ZEDONG ANNOUNCED THE PEOPLE'S REPUBLIC OF CHINA,
fourteen separate political parties were represented in the government. But China was actually ruled by the CCP, with Mao as its chairman. He headed a party of about 4.5 million members, 90 percent of whom were peasants. Mao's right-hand-man, Zhou Enlai, was named the nation's prime minister.

The CCP regime began at once to create a "new China." Mao and party leaders were determined to set up a classless society. As Mao explained, "When classes disappear, all instruments of class struggle—parties and the state machinery—will lose their function, cease to be necessary . . . human society will move to a higher stage. We are the opposite of the political parties of the bourgeoisie."

To Communists, the bourgeoisie are capitalists, a class of people who control the means of production (factories, tools, machinery, for

THE PEOPLE'S REPUBLIC

AT THE BEGINNING OF THE PEOPLE'S REPUBLIC OF CHINA, MAO *(LEFT)* **WAS** named chairman and Zhou Enlai *(right)* was named China's prime minister. They were the two most powerful men in the country.

example) and employ wage laborers. Communist ideology accused the bourgeoisie of taking advantage of workers and creating wealth primarily for themselves. Communist cadres—groups of loyal CCP members—spread this propaganda throughout China, particularly among the proletariat and the peasants.

Before progress could be made toward a classless society, the country had to tackle numerous problems that had developed because of the long civil war. Many industries had been destroyed. Unemployment was high in the cities. There were food shortages, and poverty was widespread. Nevertheless, beginning in the 1950s, Mao and his leaders initiated mass movements and campaigns to change China's social and economic order. Mao made it clear he would follow the pattern of the Soviet Union. "The

THE LONG CIVIL WAR LEADING UP TO MAO'S TAKEOVER OF CHINA LEFT many Chinese, such as this group in Shanghai, in poverty.

Communist Party of the Soviet Union is our best teacher and we must learn from it," he said.

Soon after the establishment of the People's Republic of China, Mao went to Moscow to negotiate with the Soviet Union's dictator Joseph Stalin (1878–1953). Mao worked out agreements for loans and advisers to help set up Chinese industries. Stalin and Mao signed a Treaty of Friendship, Alliance, and Mutual Assistance in February 1950. The treaty provided the requested money and advisers for China.

A "DEMOCRATIC DICTATORSHIP"

Mao preached that peasants, the working class, and the Communist Party would enforce a "dictatorship over . . . the landlord class and bureaucrat–bourgeoisie" (those linked to the KMT) as well as reactionaries—people against radical social or political change. To bring about a classless society, a democratic dictatorship was necessary, he said, because a "people's state" had to be set up first with a "people's army, people's police and the people's court." Otherwise the revolution would fail. He declared:

> Only when the people have such a state can they educate and remould themselves on a country-wide scale by democratic methods and, with everyone taking part, shake off the influence of domestic and foreign reactionaries . . . rid themselves of bad habits and ideas acquired in the old

society, not allow themselves to be led astray by the reactionaries, and to continue to advance . . . towards a socialist and communist society.

THE KOREAN WAR

Just as the new society was forming, China again was at war, this time in Korea, the peninsula along China's eastern border. For decades, Korea had been under the control of Japan, and during World War II, the Allies (which included the United States, Great Britain, and the Soviet Union) had promised to free Korea when the Axis powers (Japan, Germany, Italy, and several other nations) were defeated.

After Japan's surrender, some Japanese troops remained in Korea, and U.S. and Soviet officials met to decide how to take control. The peninsula was divided at the 38th parallel of north latitude, cutting it almost in half. The Soviets occupied the North, while the United States occupied the South.

The Soviet Red Army marched into North Korea. They set up a provisional government run by Korean Communists with support from the Soviets and from China.

Numerous efforts were made to unify Korea, but all failed. Communists in the north established the Democratic People's Republic of Korea (DPRK). An election was held, but only Communists were allowed to vote. Kim Il Sung, who was supported by the USSR, became premier (leader). In the South, Syngman Rhee, who was educated in the United States and backed by the U.S. government, won election as president of the Republic of Korea (ROK).

KIM IL SUNG *(LEFT)* **BECAME THE LEADER OF THE DEMOCRATIC PEOPLE'S**
Republic of Korea, or North Korea, in 1948. Syngman Rhee *(right)* became the
leader of the Republic of Korea, or South Korea, that same year.

U.S. occupying forces pulled out, but military advisers stayed to support the new ROK army.

Communist and non-Communist parties in the North and South
made efforts toward a unified Korea. But neither side was willing to
compromise. Government officials on each side of the 38th parallel
warned their people that they would be invaded. Troops guarded
their own borders to protect the North from the South and the South
from the North.

In late June 1950, North Korean troops invaded the South.
Under the direction of the recently created United Nations (UN),
the United States and many other countries came to South Korea's
aid. UN forces pushed the North Koreans back into North Korea,

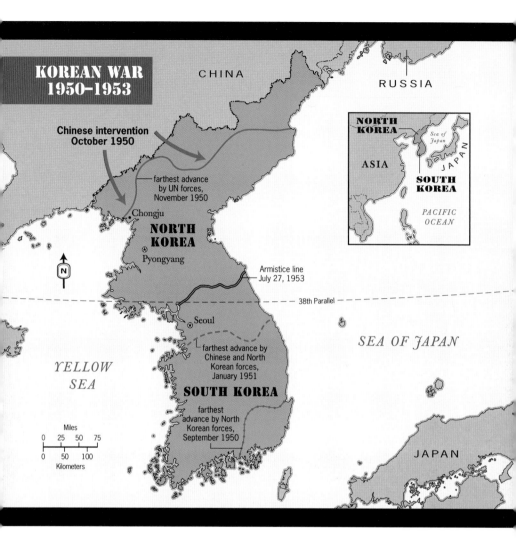

KOREAN WAR
1950–1953

CHINA

RUSSIA

Chinese intervention
October 1950

NORTH KOREA

Sea of Japan

ASIA

JAPAN

SOUTH KOREA

PACIFIC OCEAN

farthest advance
by UN forces,
November 1950

Chongju

NORTH
KOREA

Pyongyang

N

Armistice line
July 27, 1953

38th Parallel

Seoul

SEA OF JAPAN

farthest advance by
Chinese and North
Korean forces,
January 1951

YELLOW
SEA

SOUTH KOREA

farthest
advance by North
Korean forces,
September 1950

JAPAN

Miles
0   25   50   75

0   50   100
Kilometers

pursuing them northward toward the Yalu River along China's border. As the U.S.-led forces approached, Mao issued an order to the army, called the Chinese People's Volunteers, "to support the Korean people's war of liberation and to resist the attacks of U.S. imperialism."

A propaganda campaign that included many posters called for

the Chinese to "Resist America and Aid Korea." Propagandists urged people to increase production and contributions for the war effort. "Altogether, more than 2,500,000 troops were sent to Korea, as well as all of China's tanks and over half its artillery and aircraft," according to Patricia Buckley Ebrey, author of *The Cambridge Illustrated History of China*. The Chinese counterattack beat back the UN forces. A long and bloody stalemate set in.

THE COLD WAR

The battle over Korea was the first time during a forty-six-year period known as the Cold War (1945–1991) that armed hostilities took place. The Cold War was a state of tension, but not outright warfare, between the United States and the Soviet Union. It began after World War II when the United States and its allies opposed the Soviet expansion in Eastern Europe. As Eastern European governments came under Communist control, the United States and the Soviets engaged in competition for worldwide support—a competition that continued until the Soviet Union collapsed in 1991.

During the Cold War, each side found a variety of ways to threaten the other—through the media, spy programs, and rivalry in advanced technology, for example. An arms race was a major factor as the United States and the Soviets built up their supplies of nuclear weapons and threatened to use them. Each side also supported wars fought by proxy countries, such as the Korean conflict with the United States aiding one side and the Soviets aiding the other. A similar situation existed during the Vietnam War of the 1960s and 1970s.

MASS CAMPAIGNS

During the Korean conflict, the United States supported the Nationalist government in exile on the island of Taiwan. The KMT continued to oppose the Communists in mainland China. This led Mao and his cadres to impose a reign of terror, using harsh discipline to maintain control. Those who were members of the KMT plus their families and friends, or even those thought to be associated with them, were rounded up and shot. The executions were part of a mass campaign to suppress counterrevolutionaries.

An estimated eight hundred thousand people were accused of being counterrevolutionaries. Many were tried and sentenced during the first half of 1951. Tens of thousands were executed, and their names became part of long lists published in daily newspapers.

An enlistee in the Chinese army, Li Changyu, was an eyewitness to various campaigns and mass movements. He saw a trial of more than three hundred counterrevolutionaries at a stadium in Shanghai noting:

The *People's Daily* reported on this public trial and mass execution in a lead article on page one with the horrific headline, "100,000 citizens watch with thunderous shouts and applause."

Along with counterrevolutionaries, PRC government officials were also terrorized. A Three Antis Campaign began in 1951 to rid the country of waste, corruption, and bureaucracy. Some Communist officials had taken bribes, embezzled funds, or provided favors for family members. During the campaign, the CCP rounded up officials accused of corruption, including army veterans. Some were executed, and others were jailed or banished from the Party or the country.

The Five Antis Campaign took place about the same time, with capitalists as targets. Industrialists and merchants were investigated. As with the earlier Three Antis Campaign, some were accused of bribery, tax evasion, fraud, and theft of government property and economic secrets. Because some capitalists were needed to maintain industry, many were spared brutal persecution.

A FIVE-YEAR PLAN

During the early 1950s, the CCP initiated its first set of plans to reduce the country's widespread poverty and to set the stage for Socialism. Called the First Five-Year Plan, it was based on the Soviet model for developing heavy industry. At the same time, China needed to produce enough food to feed its growing population. In the CCP's view, that meant collectivizing agriculture—that is, creating a state structure for producing food. Peasants would have to give up private lands and live and work on state-owned farms known as collectives.

Writing for *China Today*, a Chinese monthly magazine, Chen Hang-sen explained in a 1955 article how

> heavy industry determines progress in every other field. This can readily be seen if we examine its connection with other fields, notably agriculture, in which the vast majority of the Chinese people are engaged. . . . Only when we can make the necessary machinery on a large scale can we have modern prosperous collective farming.

After seeing a Soviet-made tractor, an elderly Chinese peasant said, "Twenty oxen ploughing for a day can't do as much as this iron ox in one shift."

By 1955 nearly all Chinese peasants lived in collectives, and the central government controlled agricultural production. Development of heavy industry also moved ahead quickly, primarily because Mao insisted that such a system would improve food production and create more markets for industrial goods. He was convinced that, as a result, the pace of industrialization would increase.

Apparently, that was the case, according to a U.S. Library of Congress report on China's First Five-Year Plan, which pointed out:

Large numbers of Soviet engineers, technicians, and scientists assisted in developing and installing new heavy industrial facilities, including many entire plants and pieces of equipment purchased from the Soviet Union. . . . In terms of economic growth the First Five-Year Plan was quite successful, especially in those areas emphasized by the Soviet-style development strategy. A solid foundation was created in heavy industry. Key industries, including iron and steel manufacturing, coal mining, cement production, electricity generation, and machine building were greatly expanded and were put on a firm, modern technological footing. Thousands of industrial and mining enterprises were constructed, including 156 major facilities. Industrial production increased at an

MAO ZEDONG *(THIRD FROM RIGHT)* **TOURS A FACTORY IN TIANJIN IN 1956.**
Mao's Five-Year Plan placed a strong emphasis on developing heavy industry.

average annual rate of 19 percent between 1952 and 1957, and national income grew at a rate of 9 percent a year.

Another report on the plan provided some data regarding industrial production. For example, from 1952 to 1957, coal production nearly doubled, from 69 million tons (63 million metric tons) to 137 million tons (124 million metric tons). Steel production rose from 1.4 million tons (1.3 million metric tons) to 5.7 million tons (5.2 million metric tons). Pig iron (crude iron, from which steel can be produced) increased nearly five times, from 2 million tons (1.9 million metric tons) to 6.3 million tons (5.8 million metric tons). Cement production doubled, from 2.9 million tons (2.6 million metric tons) to 5 million tons (4.6 million metric tons).

Mao proclaimed the First Five-Year Plan successful. Goals had been met ahead of schedule, and few counterrevolutionaries remained to challenge the system. He believed that Socialism had triumphed over capitalism, and he apparently felt secure enough to allow a more open society.

Frank Moraes, editor of the Times of India, *was one of the few foreign observers to visit China while Mao was in power. In 1952, under strict supervision, he was able to inspect factories, mills, and mines, traveling by train to varied locations. Moraes found that as in other dictatorships, "Punctuality is a totalitarian virtue. Mao's trains run on time. You could set your watch by a Chinese train."*

HUNDRED FLOWERS AND ANTI-RIGHTIST CAMPAIGNS

In a May 1956 speech before CCP leaders, Mao surprised his listeners by declaring that there should be more input from intellectuals, such as writers and people in the arts. He called for a Hundred

Flowers Campaign, which used the slogan "let a hundred flowers blossom and a hundred schools of thought contend." The movement was supposed to be an opportunity for intellectuals and artists to help the CCP correct its faults.

Some historians contend that Mao wanted to give intellectuals a free voice in order to avert possible anti-Communist demonstrations as had taken place against the Soviet Union in Eastern Europe. Others argue that Mao deliberately planned to weed out enemies of the state—"coax the snakes out of their holes," as he told his personal physician Li Zhisui. Whatever the motivation, Mao began efforts to encourage criticism of the CCP.

However, CCP officials were not eager to carry out this campaign, which they believed would be turned against them. This led Mao in early 1957 to call for intellectuals to present their views. The result was a great deal of serious criticism. Some critics on college campuses even went so far as to create large wall posters attacking the CCP and Mao himself.

The attacks soon brought an end to the Hundred Flowers Campaign. Those who had spoken out were labeled "rightists," and an Anti-Rightist Campaign began in mid-May 1957. Thousands of rightists were sent to prison or labor camps or were executed. One victim, army reporter Dai Huang, noted that fewer than one hundred people were targeted at first. "But the campaign was expanded to cover 552,912 people," according to party documents. The campaign effectively silenced most Chinese. But an even more destructive force was beginning to ravage the country—a famine which caused widespread death from starvation and was partly the result of the second five-year plan known as the Great Leap Forward.

THE GREAT LEAP FORWARD (GLF) BEGAN IN 1958. The plan called for the rapid growth of agricultural and industrial production. Implementing this campaign, CCP officials believed, would bring about economic and technical development in great leaps, rather than at a gradual pace.

In a program more ambitious than anything ever seen before in history, the entire nation was called to action. Virtually every Chinese citizen would take part in the GLF, from the lowliest peasant to the highest-ranking CCP members.

Mao expected China to equal or exceed the industrial output of Great Britain and also the United States. After a trip around the country, he declared in an interview with a reporter, "I have witnessed the tremendous energy of the masses. On this foundation it is possible to accomplish any task whatsoever."

OF DEATHS

MASSIVE COLLECTIVIZATION

The vast majority of the rural population was organized into communes. Unlike earlier stages of land reform where farmers pooled their property in small collectives, the commune system was a much larger operation. Each commune took over ownership of what private land remained and developed its own collective farm, small manufacturing facilities, and construction projects.

A commune was made up of production brigades of several hundred households. The brigades were divided into teams of twenty to forty or more households. The brigade set up workshops and schools, while the teams organized farm laborers.

The CCP issued instructions on what would be produced and

how crops would be planted and harvested. In addition, all members of the commune were required to eat their meals in canteens (communal dining areas). People were not allowed to cook in their homes, and some families hated the canteens. Yet, for the first time in their lives, many farmworkers were able to eat as much as they wanted. They felt secure because the state supplied everything, including kitchen utensils and cooking pots for the canteens.

MAKING STEEL

The GLF also included mandatory industrialization. People across the nation were organized to produce steel. Planners believed this single commodity would allow industries to develop and manufacture heavy machinery.

On Mao's orders, people in the communes as well as in city neighborhoods set up backyard furnaces to melt down scrap metal for iron and steel production. The goal was to double the output of steel within a year. Families tossed their cooking utensils, pots, iron bedsprings, metal doorknobs and hinges, railings, farm tools, and almost any cast-iron items they owned or found into the furnaces.

Everyone was urged to help make steel—even young children. When author Jung Chang was six years old, she collected scrap iron objects as she walked to and from school. She recalled:

> I screwed up my eyes to search every inch of ground for broken nails, rusty cogs, and any other metal. . . . In my school, cruciblelike vats had replaced some of our cooking

woks and were sitting on the giant stoves in the kitchen. All our scrap iron was fed into them. . . . Our teachers took turns feeding firewood into [the furnaces] around-the-clock, and stirring the scraps in the vats with a huge spoon.

With so much emphasis on steel output as well as on development of other small industries and building projects, people were pulled away from agriculture. Crop production began to falter. But Mao was adamant about increasing agricultural output, and communes were expected to meet high quotas or face punishment. So CCP cadres and many peasants exaggerated their harvests. There were claims that gigantic vegetables—cabbages, cucumbers, tomatoes—and millions of pounds of potatoes and huge volumes of grain had been produced.

AS PART OF MAO'S GREAT LEAP FORWARD, CHINESE WORKERS OPERATED
backyard blast furnaces to melt steel from everyday metal items.

In addition, government planners without agricultural expertise were the ones who determined farming methods, and they dictated the use of Soviet techniques that had failed years earlier. For example, they ordered peasants to plant their crops close together to increase productivity. When plants sprouted, they appeared healthy. But as densely planted crops grew, they did not get enough nutrients from the soil. The result was massive crop failures.

Another CCP order required the extermination of sparrows. The small birds were thought to carry diseases related to poor hygiene that affected many peasants. People took great pride in killing the birds and parading down the street with their carcasses. Actually, the birds ate insects that were crop pests. When the

PEASANTS TOIL IN THE FIELDS DURING THE GREAT LEAP FORWARD.
Virtually the entire Chinese population was mobilized during this time.

sparrows were chased away or killed, insects multiplied and severely damaged plants. Again, agricultural production suffered. The results of these mistakes were catastrophic.

A FAILED PLAN

Some major communal efforts during the Great Leap Forward were successful. They included the construction of canals, irrigation systems, and roads. One huge undertaking was a water conservation project that involved one hundred million peasants. But the GLF had adverse economic effects and took a great toll on human life. Some historians have called the plan a complete failure.

Evidence of foolhardy efforts and lack of technical knowledge included the backyard furnaces. They produced steel of inferior quality. It was brittle and useless for many building projects or contributed to the collapse of some structures.

In addition, the inflated reports of agricultural production led the CCP to send many farmers to work in industries. Meanwhile, crops rotted in the fields. At the same time, much of the grain (reported as a surplus) was diverted from rural to urban areas. It was kept in storage or exported to other countries to fund industrial programs. By 1959 people in the cities and countryside were suffering from scarcity of food.

Between 1959 and the end of 1961, China suffered a terrible famine, the worst in world history. Although food shortages for the most part were directly related to the policies of the Great Leap Forward, natural disasters—a major flood and drought in some areas—also played a role.

An estimated twenty million to forty million people died of starvation. Because the Chinese government kept details of the famine secret for decades, few Western nations knew about this tragedy. Even when Chinese travelers or refugees who fled to Hong Kong (then under British colonial rule) described conditions in the nation, they were usually ignored or thought to be exaggerating. One report noted that eyewitnesses "spoke of food shortage and hunger; swollen bellies, lack of protein and liver diseases were common. Many babies were stillborn because of their mothers' deficient nutrition. . . . In Shenyang the newspaper reported cannibalism. Desperate mothers strangled children who cried for food."

However, such accounts were ridiculed by some in the European and American press. British author Edgar Snow, who had written such a favorable assessment of Mao in the 1930s, traveled through China in 1960. Snow, like some other foreign visitors, accepted the government's claim that the country's agricultural production was increasing. However, as Jung Chang and coauthor Jon Halliday report, "Mao told barefaced lies" about the famine and "he was widely believed." When dignitaries from France, Canada, Britain, and the United Nations visited China, they were "duped," the authors declared.

In spite of clear evidence in cities, villages, and the countryside of starving people, "no one was ever allowed to mention publicly or privately that there was a famine or even hint at the fact. Propaganda encouraged people to make a virtue out of eating less," according to Jasper Becker, a journalist. In the mid-1990s, Becker interviewed hundreds of survivors of the famine and found that "the horror of the famine [was] indelibly imprinted on their memories."

Dali Yang, who was born after the GLF ended and grew up in China, heard stories from his parents about the horrors of the famine. "Had there been a free press and other institutions of oversight that are commonly found in open political systems, the Great Leap famine would certainly not have attained the magnitude it did," he told a reporter for the *University of Chicago Chronicle*.

As people tried to find food and survive, some left the communes and began farming on their own. Rural militias (groups of citizen soldiers) formed to protect food supplies or to seize grain where it was available. Turmoil reigned in the countryside, and the CCP feared that it would lose power and be unable to control the nation.

A CHINESE-SOVIET SPLIT

During the famine years, the relationship between China and the Soviet Union deteriorated. The Soviet dictator Stalin had died in 1953. Mao believed he should have been chosen the leader of the world's Communists. But the man who eventually succeeded Stalin, Nikita Khrushchev (1894–1971), did not share that view.

Khrushchev had little regard for Mao and his admiration of Stalin. In fact, Khrushchev personally denounced Stalin and began to make changes in his country. For example, he released political prisoners, relaxed censorship of the media, and attempted to ease tensions with the United States.

All of this Mao viewed with disdain, and he accused Khrushchev of discarding Communist principles. Mao believed the Soviets were becoming too friendly with "imperialists."

After Khrushchev visited China in 1958 and 1959, he criticized Mao's plan for creating communes. Khrushchev more or less called

SOVIET LEADER NIKITA KHRUSHCHEV *(RIGHT)* **MEETS WITH MAO ZEDONG** during Khrushchev's 1958 visit to China. The relationship between the two countries worsened over the next few years.

the effort a dreamer's vision of an ideal state in an economically backward country. About the same time, Khrushchev pulled all of the Soviet technicians and advisers out of China and greatly reduced economic aid. It was the beginning of a split between Soviet Communism and Chinese Communism.

GLF CRITICS

Some CCP officials tried to tell Mao about the problems brought on by the GLF. But Mao refused to listen at first. He kept insisting that all was going well with his plan.

One critic was Mao's longtime comrade, Peng Dehuai, the minister of defense. Peng had always been a fearless army leader and loyal to the CCP. Despite this, Mao rejected Peng's criticism and denounced him, replacing him with Lin Biao.

However, Mao eventually had to admit that the GLF was a failure. At a party meeting, he said, "The main responsibility was mine, and you should take me to task. Who was responsible for the idea of the mass smelting of steel? I say it was me. . . . The chaos caused was on a grand scale, and I take responsibility. Comrades, you must all analyze your own responsibility." Party leaders forced Mao to resign as head of the government. He continued as chairman of the Chinese Communist Party, but his power was diminished.

Liu Shaoqi became head of state. He, Zhou Enlai, and Deng Xiaoping took charge of the People's Republic of China. The trio initiated more moderate policies than Mao had put in place. To help bring China out of an economic depression, the new leadership ended the GLF. The size of communes was reduced so that they could be managed better. In addition, peasants were allowed to own some land and resume "sideline production"—buying and selling activities that could supplement their farming incomes. Peasants could harvest surplus food and sell it, to buy other goods they needed.

Although Mao apparently agreed that the economy had to be fixed, he did not take his loss of influence lightly. Even powerful dictators need the support of high-ranking political and military officials—as well as support from the general public—to remain in power. Mao stayed in the background for a time, but he began to suspect that Chinese government leaders were following the pattern of Soviet "revisionists" who no longer were truly committed to revolution and Communist principles. Many times he promoted his view that an endless class struggle was basic to a Socialist society. He would use this issue as a means to regain his power.

Mao brought together a group of radicals, including his fourth wife, Jiang Qing, an actress he married after sending He Zizhen to the Soviet Union in 1937 for psychiatric treatment. Mao never formally divorced He before marrying Jiang. The radicals strongly criticized party officials thought to be corrupting the revolution and taking the "capitalist road." By 1966 Mao had regained enough influence to announce at a meeting of the CCP Central Committee a plan called the Great Proletarian Cultural Revolution, or simply the Cultural Revolution. It would be a new effort to create a China in line with Mao's thinking.

GREAT PROLETARIAN CULTURAL REVOLUTION

The stated purpose of the Cultural Revolution was to revitalize the values of Communism and bring about a classless society. To Mao this meant eliminating any remnants of past culture, customs, ideas, and habits. He called these the Four Olds and ordered them destroyed.

Meanwhile, Mao maneuvered to remove Liu Shaoqi from office. Liu was imprisoned and tortured to death. Deng Xiaoping was sent to a remote factory and kept under guard. Zhou Enlai, a skilled politician, was allowed to stay within the party and remained premier but with limited power.

Mao enlisted Chinese youth to launch the Cultural Revolution. They ranged in age from twelve to thirty, but most were uniformed teenage students. They wore red armbands and became known as Red Guards. At first only "good class" young people from peasant, cadre, worker, or military families were allowed to join. A million Red Guards gathered in Tiananmen Square in August 1966 to listen to Mao and receive their marching orders, so to speak. They rallied in the square eight more times between August and November 1966.

The Red Guards were ordered to expose and condemn intellectuals, as well as anyone with connections to the Western world who might be suspected of being a capitalist sympathizer. "Everybody wanted to join the Red Guards because nobody wanted to be 'unqualified,' 'backward' and 'non-revolutionary,'" wrote Mo Bo, who was fourteen years old when the Cultural Revolution reached his school. "I was one of the first to join because, being from a poor peasant's family, my background was supposed to be 'clear.'"

CHINESE YOUTH RALLY IN TIANANMEN SQUARE IN 1966. THEY ARE HOLDING up copies of the *Little Red Book* by Mao Zedong.

Most schools were closed indefinitely, and students received free transportation and food to travel across the nation to spread Mao's ideas and to punish "capitalist roaders." Wherever the Red Guards went, they quoted Mao's words published in *Quotations from Chairman Mao Zedong*, more commonly known as the *Little Red Book*. They carried and brandished the *Little Red Book*, and they held "struggle meetings"—public gatherings to criticize and humiliate people whom they suspected were capitalist advocates.

A long article in the *Peking Review* in September 1966 praised the Red Guards' activities, saying, "With the revolutionary rebel spirit of the proletariat, they have launched a furious offensive to sweep away reactionary, decadent bourgeois and feudal influences, and all old ideas, culture, customs and habits. This mounting revolutionary storm is sweeping the cities of the entire nation." The article declared that with the support of workers and the PLA, the "great proletarian cultural revolution will be carried through to complete victory."

RED GUARD ATTACKS

In their "revolutionary rebel spirit," the Red Guards trashed temples, museums, and theaters. They gathered books and burned them, and destroyed priceless art objects and musical instruments. Frequently, they raided homes, confiscating furniture, clothing, jewelry, and any items that reflected the Four Olds.

Ji-Li Jiang, in her memoir, *Red Scarf Girl*, tells about the Red Guard attacks that she and her family endured. The Jiangs were Communists, and Ji-Li had dreams of becoming a Red Guard. But the family was denounced because Ji-Li's father had been born into a wealthy landlord family. Her father was sent to a labor camp, and her elderly grandmother was ordered to sweep alleyways "like the other landlords' wives." The Jiang house was raided, leaving only "a barren warehouse. Our beds were straw mats on the floor. Our few clothes were in a packing crate. . . . Our table was the lid of a crate laid across two benches," Jiang wrote.

Often entire families like the Jiangs were labeled "enemies of the people" simply because of the jobs or positions the adults held or had held a generation earlier. Once labeled, people were forced to criticize themselves in public. Sometimes they were paraded through the streets in dunce caps or they were held for long periods

MANY CHINESE WERE PERSECUTED BOTH PUBLICLY AND PRIVATELY DURING
the Cultural Revolution. These Red Guards force some citizens to stand on ladders and hold signs as punishment for being leaders of so-called "anti-revolutionary groups" in Beijing.

of time in the painful "jet-plane position," with head pushed down and arms raised up. Severe beatings were common.

Teachers were some of the first victims of the Cultural Revolution. As Mo Bo put it, "We all enjoyed having no classes and degrading the teachers."

Wang Yinju was one teacher who became a victim. She was married and pregnant at the time of the Cultural Revolution. Forty years later, she recalled the terror she endured:

One day, my very own students came and dragged me out from my dormitory to the quadrangle, tied me up and put a sign board around my neck. One of them poured a bottle of black ink over my head to humiliate me. I was kicked, punched and forced to discredit myself. For the next three days, I was humiliated in front of all other school children. If not for some parents who tried to stop their children from carrying on with the brutal behavior, I probably would have died there.

Although Wang survived to tell her story, she lost her child during her ordeal. Some victims were permanently injured or mutilated and murdered. Others suffered such severe abuse and long imprisonment that they committed suicide.

DISORDER AND CHAOS

As Red Guard squads formed across the country, factions developed. Each group claimed to be more loyal to Mao than the other.

Dozens of groups battled one another in various cities, using guns they had stolen from army garrisons. The result was disorder, chaos, and many dead and wounded.

In many areas, local party officials who were attacked by Red Guards armed themselves to fight back. Factory and shipyard workers, who had been striking in cities to increase their wages and improve their working conditions, joined the fray. So did railroad workers. The strikes disrupted transportation and created economic turmoil.

Premier Zhou Enlai attempted to mediate between various revolutionary factions and to establish an atmosphere of normalcy. Meanwhile, Mao began to reevaluate the Cultural Revolution and the ongoing violence. He realized the country was on the verge of civil war and called for the PLA to intervene. The army broke up strikes and dispersed the Red Guards. The PLA arrested many Red Guard leaders and sent them to the countryside to work in the fields.

In 1969, when the CCP held its Ninth National Party Congress, the Cultural Revolution ended, and Mao became the leader of the CCP once again. Lin Biao was named his successor. But the party was not united. Two main factions—radicals (or leftists) and moderates—maneuvered for control. Defense Minister Lin Biao led the leftists, and Premier Zhou Enlai led the moderates. Mao played both sides. He believed that the zeal of the radicals was necessary to obtain a classless society. At the same time, he understood that the moderates were needed to modernize the economy and bring stability to the nation. Regardless, the factional struggles had benefited him greatly. While each side had been weakened, Mao himself had regained his position of power.

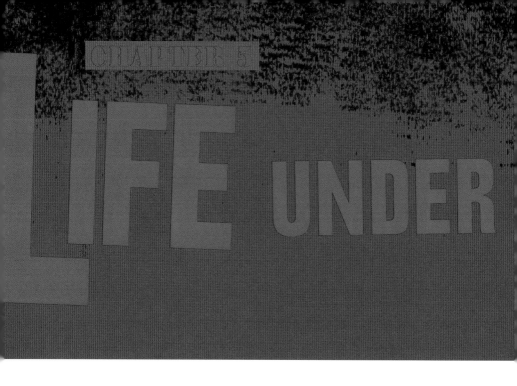

CHAPTER 5

LIFE UNDER

FROM THE BEGINNING OF MAO'S DICTATORSHIP through the Cultural Revolution and beyond, CCP officials applied Mao's theory that people's lives had to be controlled by the government. This was accomplished by fear, murderous terror campaigns, and by managing public opinion through propaganda methods—speeches, posters, directives, published materials, and theatrical performances.

Most of the propaganda messages came from Mao himself. People frequently quoted his words and were eager to show their devotion to him. Many of his followers—especially peasants and workers—were convinced that he cared about them, and Mao's speeches and writings were designed to give that impression. Yet, after extensive interviews and research, authors Jung Chang and Halliday concluded that Mao never was truly concerned about the welfare of peasants. Rather, he organized and used illiterate and

MAO'S
DICTATORSHIP

RED GUARDS LINE UP IN FRONT OF A PORTRAIT OF MAO IN BEIJING IN THE late 1960s. Mao's picture was ever present at important events and places throughout China during the Cultural Revolution.

poverty-stricken farmers as agitators to stir up the poor against the rich in villages. And he had no qualms about sacrificing them— starving and working them to death—in campaigns such as the Great Leap Forward.

MEDIA ROLES

Mao's writings were among the most effective forms of media to spread CCP propaganda. Lin Biao, the defense minister who had published the *Little Red Book*, encouraged the "cult of Mao," as it became known. Lin used the People's Liberation Army to reinforce the image of Mao as a god or revered emperor. He made certain that the PLA was loyal to Mao and that soldiers studied Mao's *Quotations*. The PLA also supervised artistic expressions such as paintings and stage performances. These had to conform to *Mao Zedong's Thought*—his official writings published in four volumes titled *Selected Works of Mao Tse-Tung* (a fifth volume was published after Mao's death).

THIS RED GUARD COVERED himself with Mao buttons during the Cultural Revolution.

Copies of Mao's writings were placed on special tables in homes and were considered sacred. Quotations from the *Little Red Book* appeared on stationery, in newspapers, and other publications. In public, people recited Mao's words and pledged allegiance to their "beloved leader." In workplaces and in public squares, people bowed before Mao's portrait. Artwork and huge posters extolled Mao and his works. People wore Mao badges. Animals were branded with the

A LETTER TO AN AMERICAN GRANDMOTHER

Mao's words saturated public places in cities, towns, villages, and the countryside. Li Min, who worked in the countryside of Henan Province in China during the late 1960s, certainly heard Mao's statements. Though Li Min seldom wrote in English, he sent a letter describing his experiences to his American grandmother. His letter is posted on the website of the Society for Anglo-Chinese Understanding (SACU), a nongovernmental agency that promotes friendship between the British and Chinese. In part, Li Min wrote:

> When night comes you can hear a lot of children are reading in our village. If you come near them, you may know they are reading Chairman Mao's works. Really they are reading for villagers. They are Red Guards. So all the villagers can study Chairman Mao's works, the Red Guard have this good idea: when night comes they standing at street, every one hundred foot a guard. The leader reads a sentence. The second guard read it again then the third read again, and so on. They just like radio station. After peasants labour all day long they can listen to Chairman Mao's works for their rest.

Chinese word for loyalty "to show that even dumb beasts could recognize Mao's genius." All of these rituals helped to elevate Mao to godlike status in the minds of his people.

In addition, the public was constantly bombarded with propaganda supporting the revolution—films, plays, paintings, and operas.

BIG-CHARACTER POSTERS

Big-character posters *(below, on pillars on a street in Guangzhou in 1966)* were part of the widespread propaganda tools of the Cultural Revolution. Called a *dazibao*, which means "big-character journal," the poster was handwritten and often included cartoons and other drawings. Such posters frequently criticized, condemned, denounced, or ridiculed individuals who were considered "capitalist roaders." They were pasted on walls, sides of buildings, doors, windows, or other surfaces and "even hung from between parasol trees, rustling like ghosts in the night," as Liang Heng put it.

Liang was a young student during the Cultural Revolution, and he took part in creating posters criticizing teachers and others. But he soon became disillusioned when big-character posters condemned his father, a loyal Communist and supporter of Mao Zedong.

Operas, in particular, were avidly promoted by Mao's wife, Jiang Qing. Revolutionary committees were set up in schools, factories, rural communes, and other workplaces to oversee daily affairs and effectively promote Communist ideals as articulated by Mao Zedong.

The media messages gave the impression that "the whole of China seemed to be marching to Mao's step," British journalist Philip Short reported.

Those who had their doubts did not dare speak out, fearing imprisonment or death. Even Mao's personal physician for twenty-two years, Dr. Li Zhisui, could not object to anything the dictator said or did. "Those of us around him had to grant his every wish," Li wrote in his memoir.

RURAL LIFE

Before the Communist takeover of China, many Chinese peasants were tenant farmers. They rented plots of land from gentry and paid their rent in crops. Some peasants also owned small plots and rented out part of their land. These people were known as semi-landlords and, like Mao's father, were able to acquire some wealth. They were called rich peasants.

Even before the new regime was established, the Red Army initiated land reform by "liberating" property. They seized it from owners and turned it over to peasants. Mao, in fact, urged peasants to rise up against the landlords and prosperous semilandlords. Mao argued that gentry frequently killed or persecuted peasants "without batting an eyelid." Thus he believed justice was served by executing landlords. He often repeated that justification and declared in a party directive, "The reactionary armed bands of the landlords and the reactionary secret police must be destroyed." However, he warned that "killing without discrimination is strictly forbidden."

An Agrarian Reform Law was passed in 1950, which was supposed to distribute landlords' property—land, farming equipment, animals, and buildings—evenly among the poor peasants, rich peasants, and landlords. Government reports claimed that 700 million mou (115.3 million acres or 46.7 million hectares) of land was divided among three hundred million peasants. The law provided for each peasant to receive a little over a third of an acre. But it was not unusual for party officials to increase the share of property for relatives and friends.

HOW LAND REFORM TOOK PLACE

To carry out the Agrarian Reform Law, CCP cadres encouraged peasants to take over the land and to set up trials, charging landlords with numerous brutal crimes. At times mob rule seemed to take over. Photographs and published accounts of these trials indicate that many peasants were eager to denounce landlords and to avenge the injustices they had suffered. It was common for peasants to spit on landlords, force them to wear or carry signs describing their "sins," and loudly criticize them in public. Then the landlords were executed.

In some cases, landlords resisted confiscation of their property by burning buildings, killing farm animals, poisoning food, destroying equipment, and attacking peasants. Those who defied the reforms faced certain death if captured. Between 1949 and 1953, as many as one million former landowners were executed, and those not put to death were sent to camps and "rehabilitated"— forced to learn about and accept the Communist policy.

Not all landlords were treated brutally or killed, however, according to Jung Chang, an eyewitness. In her book *Wild Swans: Three Daughters of China*, Chang tells of her and her family's life in China, where they were members of the Communist Party. Her father ran the reform program in the Yibin area of Sichuan Province. In Sichuan, reform "was on the whole nonviolent, partly because the fiercer landlords had been involved in the rebellions during the first nine months of Communist rule and had already been killed in battle or executed," Chang wrote. Landlords in the province who cooperated or helped the Communists suffered the loss of their property but not necessarily physical harm.

Jung Chang described some vicious incidents, however. In one, a party member "raped the female members of a landowner's family and then mutilated them by cutting off their breasts." Her father ordered the man's execution.

Another episode involved an outlaw group called a bandit gang. Such gangs were semimilitary operations led by warlords, and their main purpose was to plunder, take over farmland and water supplies, and brutally force farmers to pay a tax for protection. One gang captured a young Communist student who was searching for food outside the city of Yibin. At the time, food supplies were scarce throughout the province. After the gang captured the student, "the chief ordered him to be cut in half," according to Jung Chang. "The chief was later caught, and beaten to death by the Communist land reform team leader."

WOMEN'S STATUS

Another reform law focused on women and their status within marriage. Over the centuries, Chinese women had few, if any, rights. Mao initiated the Marriage Reform Law of 1950, which freed many women from subservient roles.

The Marriage Reform Law banned practices that had been followed since ancient times. Men were no longer allowed to keep concubines—women who were bought or given to them but were not legal marriage partners. Men were also forbidden to have multiple wives. Marriage reform meant that the patriarch (male leader of the family) did not have to be recognized as the authority in the household. Arranged marriages were prohibited as well. Men and women could freely choose their mates, and both genders gained equal rights to file for divorce.

Reporter Frank Moraes, who was in China at the time, wrote: "Of the many changes noticeable under the Red regime few strike the visitor more than the altered status of women." He added that with "feminine emancipation, China has at one vault leaped several centuries."

Along with the new marital rights, women obtained new equality under land reform. Previously women had no right to own land, but the Agrarian Reform Law changed that. Men no longer held ownership of all the land. Women were allowed their equal share of the soil that they helped farm. They also had the right to determine whether and how land would be sold.

Women worked alongside men in factories and mills. In the early 1950s, Frank Moraes reported, "Some 650,000 women workers are employed in various industries. These comprise scientists,

IN THE LATE 1960S, THE LI SE YUAN MINE EMPLOYED BOTH MEN AND women as coal miners. These men and women are reading from Mao's *Little Red Book* during the Cultural Revolution.

technicians, engineers, factory managers and directors, tram drivers, train conductors, train crews and ordinary industrial workers." In addition, he noted, "There are women in the people's army, navy, and air forces. . . . At least 600,000 women rank as members of the Chinese Communist Party."

FOREIGN AFFAIRS

While domestic matters took center stage during the 1950s, foreign affairs, especially the deteriorating relationship with the Soviets, could not be ignored. Khrushchev was more than just critical of Mao and China's Great Leap Forward. He and the Soviets became incensed during the 1960s when Red Guards harassed Soviet diplomats during the Cultural Revolution.

Then in 1969, China faced armed conflict with the Soviet Union on the northeastern and western Chinese-Soviet border. Fears of war led to increased searches for and persecution of those considered traitors to the revolutionary cause. To prevent major battles, Zhou Enlai met with Soviet premier Aleksey Kosygin, and both sides pulled back, although troops remained on the border.

Meanwhile, the Cold War became a "hot war" in Vietnam, China's neighbor. Like Korea nearly a decade earlier, Vietnam had

CHINESE AND SOVIET SOLDIERS CLASH AT THE BORDER BETWEEN THE TWO countries in February 1969. In March the dispute escalated to a firefight.

been divided between a Communist North and non-Communist South. In 1961 U.S. president John F. Kennedy (1917–1963) sent U.S. troops to South Vietnam, to assist the South Vietnamese in their fight against the North. After Kennedy was assassinated in 1963, his successor, Lyndon B. Johnson (1908–1973), sent more U.S. forces to Vietnam, as did the next president, Richard M. Nixon (1913–1994).

The Chinese were aiding the Vietnamese in their fight against U.S.-backed forces. But Mao knew that he could not challenge both the United States and the Soviet Union at the same time. Since he did not trust the Soviet Union, he decided that the United States was a lesser threat. Improving relations with the United States might strengthen Mao's claim to being the leading figure in world Communism. It might also show that Mao was a "major foreign-policy decision-maker," as China expert Jonathan Spence put it.

TO CHINA VIA TABLE TENNIS

U.S. access to China occurred in a roundabout fashion through table tennis, more popularly known as Ping-Pong. In April 1971, the World Table Tennis Championship was being held in Nagoya, Japan. A U.S. team was taking part in the contest, as were teams from China. While in Japan, the Americans received an astonishing invitation from the Chinese to visit the People's Republic of China, all expenses paid. No U.S. group had been welcomed in China since Mao Zedong's regime had taken over in 1949.

The Americans were participants in exhibition matches between the Chinese and U.S. teams. In addition, they were escorted by

Chinese officials to such famous sites as the Great Wall and the Summer Palace outside of Beijing. Before the end of the weeklong visit, Premier Zhou Enlai hosted a reception at the Great Hall of the People in Beijing for the Americans and other guest teams. Zhou reportedly told the U.S. players that after a "long period of severance," their visit had "opened the door to friendship between the peoples of the two countries."

A MEMBER OF THE TEAM

Judy Hoarfrost *(opposite page, seventh from right)* recalled her experiences as the youngest member of the U.S. table-tennis team playing at the 1971 world championship matches in Japan. At the time, she was only fifteen years old and called her visit "a great adventure."

A resident of Oregon, Hoarfrost spoke to a group celebrating "China Week" at Texas A&M University at College Station, Texas. She described the practice sessions at the Japanese Aichi Stadium. "It was very noisy with people talking. All of a sudden a hush came over the whole stadium. I looked up and saw the Chinese team marching in. Everyone stood in awe, because they were the gods of table tennis for us."

In China her experiences were no less awesome, especially when she met Premier Zhou in the Great Hall of the People. "The U.S. delegation sat in a conference room with delegations from other countries who had also been invited to China after the World Championship. . . . Upon entering the hall, we each shook hands with the premier," Hoarfrost told a reporter. On her return to the United States, she learned that she had

Zhou's words were not just idle talk. Almost immediately the U.S. government revoked a twenty-year embargo (ban) against trade with China. And the following year, the Chinese table tennis team visited the United States, playing in exhibition matches and touring the country. The matches, both in China and the United States, quickly became known as Ping-Pong diplomacy—one outward sign that the two governments might develop some type of alliance.

become a celebrity, and photographs of her handshake with the premier had appeared in newspapers worldwide.

NIXON AND MAO

When Richard M. Nixon was elected in 1968 as the thirty-seventh U.S. president, he was well known as an anti-Communist and had expressed his hostility toward China. But he was aware that China might help to end the Vietnam War and assist the United States in efforts to curb Soviet power. He carefully sent various signals that the United States wanted to improve relations with China.

One such gesture was lifting the trade embargo after the table-tennis exhibitions. Another was easing a ban on American travel to China. One more signal was a statement by Secretary of State William Rogers that the United States wanted to "open up channels of communication."

Mao began to send his own messages of possible contact with the West. When author Edgar Snow visited China again in 1970, Mao referred to President Nixon's comment that had appeared in a *Time* magazine article. Nixon had said: "If there is anything I want to do before I die, it is to go to China." Mao asked Snow to relay a response saying, "I would be happy to talk with him [Nixon], either as a tourist or as President."

Snow's message never reached the White House. But before the end of 1971, Nixon's national security adviser, Henry Kissinger, was making secret plans for the president's visit to China. The arrangements were not disclosed to the American public because of the years of animosity between China and the United States. The idea of dealing with Communists would shock Americans as well as the United States' allies. Still, Nixon knew that his longtime anti-Communist stance would help shield him from accusations of being soft on the country's Cold War enemies.

At first Nixon attempted to establish contacts with China through diplomatic contacts in Poland. When that did not work out, the president and Kissinger decided to seek help from Pakistan, which had friendly relations with both China and the United States. The Pakistani president conveyed messages back and forth from Nixon to Mao and their representatives.

Kissinger eventually held a meeting with Zhou Enlai in mid-1971. Afterward, Kissinger sent a five-page memorandum to Nixon, explaining in detail his and Zhou's comments, reactions, and how each nation's agenda was presented and received. The memo was classified top secret for decades but was made public as part of a 2004 National Security Archives documentary titled *Declassified: Nixon in China*. Available on the Internet, Kissinger's memo begins: "My two-day visit to Peking [Beijing] resulted in the most searching, sweeping and significant discussions I have ever had in government."

A few days after Kissinger returned to the United States, President Nixon announced on a television program that he would be going to China in early 1972. Over the following months, Kissinger made several more trips to China and completed the arrangements.

NIXON'S VISIT

In February 1972, Nixon flew on the presidential plane to the Beijing Airport, where he and his wife, Pat, were greeted by Zhou Enlai. It was a historic moment. Nixon was the first sitting U.S. president to visit China. He called his trip "the week that changed the world." Indeed, this was apparent when the *People's Daily* and other newspapers in China carried photographs and stories about

MAO _(LEFT)_ GREETS PRESIDENT RICHARD M. NIXON DURING THEIR HISTORIC
summit meeting in February 1972. It was the first visit ever by a U.S. president
to China.

Nixon's stay, an exceptional event for CCP-controlled news. The publication of the stories clearly indicated that the two nations, which had long been enemies, had entered an era of détente (a relaxation of tensions).

During his time in China, Nixon held frank talks with Mao and Zhou, and the Chinese cordially received the Americans. An important document called the Shanghai Communiqué outlined the relationship between the two countries. Although differences in the two countries were noted, both nations agreed that they should conduct their relations on the principles of respect for the sovereignty and territorial integrity of all states, non-aggression against other states, non-interference in the internal affairs of other states, equality and mutual benefit, and peaceful coexistence. . . . The United States and the People's Republic of China are prepared to apply these principles to their mutual relations.

The agreement also called for cultural and scientific exchanges, increased trade, and improved diplomacy.

POWER STRUGGLES

ALTHOUGH NIXON'S VISIT WAS A SUCCESS, Mao still had to deal with struggles for power within the CCP. Those struggles had focused on policy differences between Lin Biao and Premier Zhou Enlai. Lin led the PLA military commanders who wanted to confront both the Soviet Union and the United States while supporting revolutionary efforts wherever they might occur. But the opposition followed the moderate views of Zhou and a majority of regional military commanders.

"Specifically, the moderate groups . . . spoke for more material incentives for the peasantry, efficient economic planning, and a thorough reassessment of the Cultural Revolution," according to a study on China published by the U.S. Library of Congress. The moderates "also advocated improved relations with the West in general and the United States in particular—if for

AND DEATHS

no other reason than to counter the perceived expansionist aims of the Soviet Union."

LIN BIAO'S FALL

To all outward appearances, Lin Biao was Mao's loyal soldier—comrade in arms, defense minister, and Communist Party vice chairman. During the Cultural Revolution, he often quoted and defended Chairman Mao's thought and party line. But by 1971, Lin's allegiance was being questioned for a variety of reasons.

Mao was displeased with Lin because Lin and his army generals would not follow strict orders. Mao was also angry because Lin had argued publicly with Jiang Qing about the direction of the CCP. In an early 1971 speech, Mao condemned Lin, who apparently by then realized that he had lost influence and might soon be purged.

Lin's family, specifically his son Lin Liguo, were outwardly opposed to Mao. The situation put Lin Biao and others in danger of being imprisoned, tortured, and killed. Lin Liguo was deputy director of the Department of Operations of the Air Force. He devised a plan to fly his father, other family members, and some army officials to the Soviet Union.

However, the plan did not succeed. The plane took off on the night of September 12–13, 1971, but crashed in Mongolia, killing all on board. No one is certain what caused the crash. Some speculate that the plane ran out of fuel. Others suggest sabotage. After Lin's death, the government issued its version of the incident, claiming that Lin had "repeatedly committed errors." The government said Lin

was not able to give up his underhanded nature. . . . He undertook antiparty activities in a planned, premeditated way with a well determined programme with the aim of taking over power, usurping the leadership of the party, the government and the army. Mao Zedong unmasked his plot and blocked the [maneuver]. Mao Zedong made efforts to recover him but Lin Biao did not change his perverse nature.

Another view was presented by Qiu Jin of Old Dominion University in Norfolk, Virginia, in her 2002 book, *The Culture of Power: The Lin Biao Incident in the Cultural Revolution*. Qiu was an eyewitness to that time in China. She argues that Lin Biao probably went along with the plan to defect in order to protect his son. Qiu writes: "Although Lin Biao was angry at Mao's condemnations, Lin did not intend to fight back. As a member of the first generation of revolutionaries, Lin's response can be understood as typical of the mindset of his peers, who had totally surrendered themselves to the party and to its virtual deification of Mao Zedong. To them, there would be no party without Mao. Without the party, they would lose their very identities."

Qiu's father, commander in chief of the air force, was among those who were victims of Mao's revenge. "Mao purged more than 1,000 senior officials at or above the rank of army commander. Hundreds, perhaps thousands, more of junior rank were also affected," Qiu reported. For years, there was no word about the fate of her own father. She and her family were placed under house arrest and sent to the countryside. In 1981 her father suddenly appeared at a political trial and was "charged with the responsibility for the disastrous Cultural Revolution. He was sentenced to 17 years in jail."

CONTINUED PARTY STRUGGLES

After Lin Biao's attempted defection, Mao felt betrayed, and some historians say he became depressed. He was left with few choices for a designated successor. He could not choose Zhou, who was aging, suffering from cancer, and too moderate for Mao's goals.

Other possibilities included someone among the Gang of Four. This radical group formed by Mao's wife, Jiang Qing, was composed of Jiang; Zhang Chunqiao, a propagandist; writer Yao Wenyuan; and Wang Hongwen, a security official in Shanghai. Jiang expected to take Mao's place, but Mao had become increasingly displeased with his wife's scheming. He knew that she wanted to be chairman of the CCP, but he informed her that she had "provoked too much enmity"—she had made too many enemies.

Neither Jiang nor any of her inner circle could prevent Mao from bringing Deng Xiaoping back into the CCP fold. Even though Deng had been banished during the Cultural Revolution, Mao accepted Deng's self-criticism and his written request "to make up for my past mistakes." In 1973 Deng was named vice premier, which meant that he would automatically become premier upon the death of Zhou. But that did not stop the infighting.

Jiang reportedly despised Deng and kept working behind the scenes to undermine him. She sent word to Mao via two of her cohorts that Deng and Zhou were plotting to usurp power. Mao did not believe the conspiracy theory at the time, but later on, in 1975, Mao once more turned on Deng and stripped him of his positions within the CCP, although he remained a member of the party. This meant Mao again had to choose a successor and vice premier.

JIANG QING

Demon. Dragon lady. Power struck. Radical. Ruthless. Schemer. Spiteful. Vile. These are just some of the terms historians and Western and Chinese commentators have used to describe Mao's fourth wife, known as Jiang Qing. She has had few defenders, other than some fiercely loyal Communists. For example, the Communist *Workers World* published an article declaring, "When the imperialists and the reactionaries speak of Jiang Qing as the most hated woman in China, they are merely venting their own hatred of a revolutionary. They pour their venom upon her precisely because she was an unflinching and devoted adherent of the cause of revolutionary communism."

Both critics and supporters agree: Madame Mao was certainly a revolutionary. She was born in Shandong Province in 1914 and joined the Communist Party in her late teenage years. The CCP paid her expenses to study theater in Shanghai, where she became an actress. She married and divorced, and was involved with an actor, Tang Na. The couple had two children. Abandoning Tang Na and their children, Jiang left Shanghai to take part in the revolutionary struggle in Yenan, where Mao Zedong had set up headquarters.

Mao had a keen interest in theater, poetry, and opera, and admired women in the arts because they had been able to free themselves from traditional roles. Mao and Jiang met in 1938 and were married the next year. Jiang was Mao's fourth wife.

Edgar Snow met Madame Mao a few months after her marriage, describing her as "a slender, attractive young woman . . . [who] played a good game of bridge and was an excellent cook." CCP leaders in Yenan were wary of Mao's new companion. It is said that a condition of their marriage was that she stay out of politics. Jiang stayed

MAO AND JIANG QING MET IN Yenan in 1938. This photo shows the couple in 1945.

in the background until the launching of the Cultural Revolution. She became leader of the cultural group within the party's Central Committee, and she determined what was acceptable proletarian opera, drama, art, and music.

According to Jiang, all artistic expression had to portray revolutionary themes, and as with other aspects of the Cultural Revolution, everything representing the Four Olds had to be destroyed. During this time, Jiang reached her peak in power and began to see herself as the next head of the CCP.

DEATHS AND MORE STRUGGLES

Cancer took the life of China's Premier Zhou Enlai in January 1976. But China's Communist-controlled newspapers gave little space to Zhou's death. Mao did not allow the traditional formal mourning period. The reasons for not honoring this head of state are conflicting. Philip Short suggests that "Mao had never felt any personal affection for Zhou." Others contend that the radical Gang of Four maneuvered to prevent a large public show of sympathy.

This angered many people who viewed Zhou as a hero. They thought he should be shown respect on Qingmingjie, a traditional festival for remembering the dead, held on April 4. During the week before the festival, people brought wreaths and poems expressing their grief over Zhou's death and placed them at the Monument to the People's Heroes in Tiananmen Square. There were so many wreaths that "they formed a vast mound, covering the base of the Monument . . . and reaching 60 feet up its sides," reported Philip Short.

The Gang of Four led by Jiang Qing denounced the gathering, calling it counterrevolutionary. They and other radicals saw the outpouring for the moderate Zhou Enlai as a criticism of the current government. They told Mao that people were actually rallying against the revolution.

Mao sent police to remove the wreaths and poems from the monument. People were ordered to leave the square. But the next day, an angry crowd returned. In speeches and demonstrations, the crowd demanded that the wreaths be put back. As people became more and more angry, a riot broke out. Police vehicles were burned. Mao then ordered army troops and police to attack the crowd. Many were beaten and arrested.

When the CCP leadership met two days later, Mao declared that the rioting was "a reactionary event." He blamed Deng Xiaoping for inciting it. At that same meeting, Mao made a surprise announcement that the next premier and vice chairman of the party would be the little-known Hua Guofeng, whom author Jung Chang described as "an ineffectual nobody."

MAO NAMED HUA GUOFENG *(ABOVE)* the next premier and vice chairman of the Communist Party of China after Zhou Enlai's death.

Deng was no longer safe in Beijing, and he fled to another province, where he was protected by friends. But the struggle between moderates, such as Deng, and radicals, such as Jiang, was not over. In fact, it intensified during the next few months as Mao became increasingly weak from his ailments.

A NATURAL DISASTER

In late July 1976, a natural disaster made the tussle for political power more severe. A major earthquake plus aftershocks shattered the industrial city of Tangshan, east of Beijing. Most of the city's buildings

IN JULY 1976, A MAJOR EARTHQUAKE AND AFTERSHOCKS DESTROYED THE city of Tangshan. Hundreds of thousands were killed, but CCP authorities refused to accept offers for aid from other nations.

were destroyed. According to official reports, more than 240,000 people died and 164,000 were injured. Other estimates put the death toll much higher—perhaps more than half a million. The tragedy prompted aid to pour in from various parts of the country. Other nations offered help, but radicals insisted that the Chinese should take care of themselves. China refused international assistance.

Certainly no sympathy was forthcoming from Madame Mao. Instead, she used the tragedy as a political tool. She declared, "There were merely several hundred thousand deaths. So what? Denouncing Deng Xiaoping concerns eight hundred million people." And the Gang of Four put up wall posters warning that Deng was trying to "exploit earthquake phobia to suppress revolution." The radical campaign even blamed Deng for problems with relief operations.

On the other hand, Hua made certain that he was seen as sympathetic toward the earthquake victims. He personally managed immense aid efforts, which gave him the opportunity to show that he was an effective leader and thus a logical successor to Mao.

The earthquake, along with Zhou's death, contributed to widespread uncertainty about what the nation would face next. Feelings of foreboding were common, especially as Mao became less visible and his public pronouncements less frequent.

THE CHAIRMAN'S PERSONAL LIFE

To millions of Chinese, Chairman Mao Zedong could do no wrong. He was worshipped, praised, quoted, and feared. But he was also seen as contradictory, decadent, demanding, paranoid, tyrannical, selfish, and unfeeling. Yet only his inner circle of high-level CCP officials, his doctors, bodyguards, and perhaps his wives knew Mao, the man.

Chairman Mao often extolled the virtues of rural peasants and industrial workers who were considered the backbone of the nation's revolution. Mao himself was frequently portrayed as being one with the masses, living a frugal, austere life. However, he enjoyed many luxuries, including Zhongnanhai, a walled compound of buildings and lakes near Tiananmen Square and the headquarters of the CCP. The compound had once been a complex for emperors. A large indoor swimming pool near Mao's living quarters was built so that he could enjoy his favorite form of exercise. He also liked to swim in the sea and rivers whenever he could. When he was seventy-three years old, he swam in the swift-flowing Yangtze River to prove his physical stamina, a highly publicized event that helped him regain his political power in the 1960s.

Along with swimming, one of Mao's diversions was opera, a traditional performing art in China, although during the Cultural Revolution operas presented only warlike themes. When Mao visited provinces other than Beijing, party leaders, aware of Mao's love of opera, made sure that performances were scheduled.

Dancing was another pastime for Mao, although such activities had been denounced by the CCP as a Western form of self-indulgence. Dancing parties attended by young, pretty women were held in a Zhongnanhai ballroom at least once a week. On these occasions, Mao danced with dozens of women and selected those with which he wanted to share his bed in a room near the dance floor.

His sexual encounters were not confined to dancing parties. "Mao's appetite for sex was enormous," according to his personal

TO DISPEL RUMORS OF FAILING HEALTH, MAO *(BOTTOM)* **SWAM WITH SOME**
attendants in the Yangtze River in July 1966.

physician, Dr. Li Zhisui. Mao was a restless and frequent traveler, and wherever he went, he would have a woman accompany him on his private train or women brought to him at his villas and guest houses throughout the country. Being sexually active was an important part of Mao's existence. He believed this would maintain his health and extend his life.

Other personal habits appeared fanatical and included his refusal to bathe and brush his teeth. Rather than take a bath, Mao had his attendants sponge him with hot towels. He cleaned his teeth by rinsing his mouth with tea, a common peasant practice and one that Mao maintained from his days growing up in a peasant family.

Even when he had problems with abscesses and decay, he would not follow his dentist's advice to properly care for his teeth.

As Mao aged, he had to cope with poor health, including heart problems; amyotrophic lateral sclerosis, a nerve and muscle disorder also known as Lou Gehrig's disease; and failing eyesight. One of his most disturbing characteristics was increasing paranoia. He became suspicious of almost everyone around him. He began to suspect that people were trying to break into his villa or attempting to poison him. His anxiety resulted in numerous moves from one place to another throughout the country and frequent purges of party members or staff.

THIS UNDATED PHOTO SHOWS Mao smiling. His refusal to brush his teeth left them blackened and rotting.

MAO'S DEATH

Mao's health steadily deteriorated in 1976. He had several heart attacks and bounced back for a short time. But his other illnesses complicated his condition. He needed assistance to stand and walk.

He was hardly able to speak and mumbled or had to write down his thoughts, which his attendant interpreted for those around him.

According to some historians, his mind was alert. Others contend the opposite was true. Yet he was able to meet with several heads of state. He also met again with Richard Nixon after he was no longer president. When Nixon visited China in February 1976, he said "it was painful to see" Mao in such poor health.

A few months later, it was obvious to those around Mao that the chairman did not have long to live. He had a major heart attack on September 2, and his personal physician reported that "Mao was awake and alert throughout the crisis and asked several times whether he was in danger. . . . No one wanted to tell the Chairman that he could die at any moment." Mao drew his last breath ten minutes after midnight on September 9, 1976. He was eighty-two years old.

MEMORIALS

The CCP Central Committee announced Mao's death over loudspeakers, and a period of ten days was set aside for mourning. As the news spread, many people wore black armbands and paid tribute in Tiananmen Square near the Gate of Heavenly Peace, where a huge portrait of Chairman Mao was on the wall.

The Central Committee issued a long obituary for newspaper publication. It declared, in part: "All the victories of the Chinese people were achieved under the leadership of Chairman Mao. . . . The radiance of Mao Tse-tung thought will forever illuminate the road of advance of the Chinese people." The obituary urged people to "carry on the cause left behind by Chairman Mao" and

CHAIRMAN MAO'S BODY LAY IN STATE ON SEPTEMBER 12, 1976, AS mourners passed by. His body was draped with a flag bearing the hammer and sickle—two symbols of Communism.

ended with the rallying cry: "Long live the great, glorious and correct Communist Party of China! Eternal glory to our great leader and teacher Chairman Mao Tse-tung!"

A memorial service for Mao was held on September 18, and a million people gathered in Tiananmen to listen to Hua give a eulogy. Elsewhere factories, trains, and ships paid tribute by blowing whistles for three minutes. People showed their respect by stopping work and standing in silence.

In the days following the memorial, party leaders argued over what should be done with Mao's body. Years earlier, the chairman had advocated cremation. As he said to the Central Committee of the CCP: "Once you're dead you shouldn't occupy any space.

CHAIRMAN MAO'S MAUSOLEUM

A year after his death, a mausoleum in Tiananmen Square *(below)* to hold Mao's embalmed body was constructed, and his preserved corpse permanently lies in state. *The Morning Sun*, a film and website about the Cultural Revolution, noted: "The mausoleum is more than a tomb, it's a grand villa."

Inside the main entrance of the building, there is a large statue of Mao seated on a marble chair. It appears to be an imitation of the Abraham Lincoln memorial in Washington, D.C. In the main room of the mausoleum, Mao's body lies in a crystal sarcophagus (a sealed glass coffin) and can be viewed. Every day the casket is brought up from an underground, earthquake-proof chamber, and at night it is lowered back to the vault.

Millions of tourists and residents visit the mausoleum each year. In 2001, on the twenty-fifth anniversary of Mao's death, the British Broadcasting Corporation reported the reaction of one visitor: "When I saw Mao's body, tears came to my eyes. I'm so happy and excited. Mao's achievements should never be forgotten."

Burn the bodies. I'll take the lead. We should all be cremated when we die. Be turned into ashes and used to fertilize the fields." However, the leaders wanted to preserve his body, believing it should be embalmed for posterity.

THE EMBALMING EXPERIMENTS

The Politburo, the most powerful group within the CCP, and Premier Hua ordered the director of Mao's medical team to take charge of the embalming. Dr. Li was aghast. He knew at the time that science in his country was not "advanced enough" to preserve a body for an indefinite period. He had no idea what to do. But he was told to find out and that he would have all the equipment he needed to proceed.

Li knew he had to be successful or his life would be endangered. Given the political turmoil in the nation, Jiang Qing and other radicals might accuse him of being a rightist or even of murdering Mao. A bit of helpful advice, however, came from a Politburo member. He suggested that a lifelike wax model of Mao be constructed to use in case the embalming went awry. Li directed experts at the Institute of Arts and Crafts to complete the task.

Dr. Li's team consulted ancient Chinese methods of embalming. Li also thought about seeking help from the Soviets. They had done similar work on the bodies of their deceased dictators, Lenin and Stalin. But that prospect was out of the question because of the poor relationship between China and the USSR. Vietnamese officials might also be a source of information, but they refused to reveal their secrets.

Finally, Li sent an assistant to the Academy of Medical Sciences library in Beijing for information. The instructions called for the injection of 4 gallons (16 liters) of formaldehyde, a colorless gas used in a solution that preserves bodies. But just in case that was not enough to do the job, Mao's doctors decided to increase the amount to 9 gallons (34 l).

"The results were shocking," Li later wrote. "Mao's face was bloated, as round as a ball, and his neck was now the width of his head. His skin was shiny, and the formaldehyde oozed from his pores like perspiration. His ears were swollen too, sticking out from his head at right angles. The corpse was grotesque."

The doctors decided to use towels and cotton to massage Mao's face and force the formaldehyde into the lower body. For more than four hours, they worked on Mao's corpse. During that time, a portion of his face broke away, and the damage had to be covered with makeup. When his head and neck appeared presentable, his bloated body was dressed with clothing slit in inconspicuous places to fit him. The Communist red flag with the hammer and sickle was spread over the corpse. Mao was ready for display.

HUA AND DENG

Hua Guofeng, who became premier after Zhou's death, took over as CCP chairman when Mao died. Hua claimed he had proof he was Mao's rightful successor, using several written statements. One in

Mao's handwriting reportedly said to Hua, "*Ni ban shi, wo fang xin*" (With you in charge, I feel at ease).

Taking charge, Hua linked himself with moderates and began purging extreme radicals from party leadership. He also planned to take action against Mao's widow, who had tried to forge documents naming herself as Mao's successor.

Within four weeks of Mao's death, on October 6, Hua called a secret meeting of the Central Committee leadership. He sent for three of the Gang of Four: Wang Hongwen, Zhang Chunqiao, and Yao Wenyuan. When the men arrived, Central Committee guards seized them. They were arrested and charged with trying to take over leadership of the party.

THE GANG OF FOUR WERE ARRESTED IN 1976, BUT THEY DID NOT STAND trial *(above)* until 1981. *From left:* Zhang Chunqiao, an associate, Wang Hongwen, Yao Wenyuan, and Jiang Qing.

Mao's former bodyguard then went to Zhongnanhai. Jiang Qing had returned there just before the death of Mao. She was arrested, and one story says that a servant spat at her as she was taken from the compound.

When news that the Gang of Four had been arrested reached the public, wall posters appeared condemning the "four dogs." For Jung Chang, the arrests brought a joyous feeling. "My rapture was widely shared," she wrote. She, her family, and friends, along with many other Chinese, celebrated. "There was so much spontaneous rejoicing," she noted.

A campaign to dishonor the Gang of Four continued until their trial in 1980. Meanwhile, Deng, who had earned stature within the CCP, gained the backing of enough officials to be restored to his positions within the party. Now political wrangling over the successes and failures of Mao Zedong's thought and the future of the CCP took center stage.

NOT LONG AFTER MAO'S DEATH, Deng Xiaoping slowly maneuvered to bring back moderate party members who had been exiled. By 1977 he had regained his CCP offices and was overshadowing Hua, who lost control and eventually resigned as CCP chairman.

Although Deng did not take over as head of the CCP, he once again became vice chairman of the Central Committee. He was also vice chairman of the Military Commission and chief of the General Staff of the People's Liberation Army, giving him a great deal of power. He was able to place his supporters in official positions in the party, thus counteracting the radicals and their zeal for continued revolution.

Deng and other leaders advocating economic reform publicly rejected some of Mao's theories, such as continuous class struggle and austere lifestyles. The Cultural Revolution slogan that it was "better to be poor under socialism than rich under capitalism" was rejected. Instead, reformers wanted to establish a modern economic system, with monetary incentives to produce goods and market them and with investments in technology to improve industry and agriculture.

However, Deng never abandoned the theory that the basis of the Chinese economy consisted of state-owned and collectively owned sectors. He pointed out that foreign investment, which is part of the capitalist system, has "a place" in China's economy, but "it accounts for only a small portion of it and thus will not change China's social system. Achievement of common prosperity characterizes socialism, which cannot produce an exploiting class."

In 1978, under Deng's direction, the Central Committee of the CCP adopted economic reforms called the Four Modernizations.

According to the plan, agriculture, industry, the military, and science and technology would be updated to help create a modern China. Deng referred to the reforms as "socialism with Chinese characteristics." By that he meant the party would adhere to Marxism and Socialism "tailored to Chinese conditions." He further explained that Socialism would advance to Communism based on the ideal:

> . . . from each according to his ability and to each according to his needs. . . . This calls for highly developed productive forces and an overwhelming abundance of material wealth. Therefore, the fundamental task for the socialist stage is to develop the productive forces. . . . As they develop, the people's material and cultural life will constantly improve.

GANG OF FOUR IMPRISONED

While reforms were under way, Jiang and the others in the Gang of Four were brought to trial in November 1980. Many reports called it a show trial, meaning that it was carefully designed to dishonor the defendants and to demonstrate that they were political outcasts. But they were also prosecuted for serious crimes: persecution of hundreds of thousands of Chinese during the Cultural Revolution and attempting to usurp government and party power. The Gang of Four was accused of forging a document that they said was Mao's will instructing that his wife be his successor.

During the trial, Jiang "gave a long and rambling two-hour defense of the Cultural Revolution," according to a report in *Time*

JIANG QING *(CENTER)* **LISTENS DURING HER TRIAL IN JANUARY 1981. SHE** was found guilty and sentenced to death. Her sentence was later commuted to life imprisonment. She was released from prison and died in 1991.

magazine. She insisted that she had acted on Mao's orders and the decisions of Premier Zhou and the CCP Central Committee. In a final blast at the court, she said she would die for the revolutionary cause and declared, "I only wish that I had several heads for you to chop off."

All the defendants were found guilty. Jiang Qing received a death sentence, which was commuted to life in prison. The same sentence was imposed on Zhang Chunqiao. Wang Hongwen was sent to prison for life; and Yao Wenyuan, for twenty years. When Jiang was led away, she supposedly yelled, "Down with revisionism!"

Jiang was released from prison in 1991 but was confined to her Beijing home under house arrest. Not long after her release, she committed suicide, hanging herself in her apartment. (Some historians say Jiang committed suicide in prison.)

EVALUATING MAO

The trial of the Gang of Four was one step in a partial downgrading of Mao, particularly for his role in the Cultural Revolution. Because people were unsure what to think about Mao's legacy, the Central Committee adopted the Resolution on Certain Questions in the History of Our Party Since the Founding of the People's Republic of China.

The document was a review of the CCP's history. It totally condemned the Cultural Revolution and called Mao's support for it a "grave" error. Nevertheless, the resolution praised the wisdom of Mao Zedong thought and gave credit to him for establishing discipline, keeping the CCP on the Communist road, and not giving in to "capitalist roaders." Mao's contributions to the party were given top priority, while his mistakes were downplayed. He was judged to be 70 percent right and 30 percent wrong.

MAO'S MODERN-DAY DEVOTEES AND CRITICS

Since 1976 the Chinese have had diverse reactions to Mao's legacy—his policies, revolutionary fervor, and leadership. In Mao's birthplace, Shaoshan, Hunan Province, people are likely to celebrate his birth with fireworks and a festival, although that was not always the case. During the 1980s, as people became more aware of Mao's cruelty and his role in the deaths of seventy million Chinese, they were not eager to praise or remember the former chairman.

LABOR CAMP HORRORS

Some of the worst aspects of the Mao legacy are the forced labor camps that still exist. Called laogai (meaning "reform through labor"), they are designed to "rehabilitate" people who do not toe the CCP line or who are imprisoned for acts against the revolution.

For millions these camps have been a death sentence. For survivors, the trauma of the camps has lasted throughout their lives. During the 1950s and 1960s, when the Great Leap Forward and the Cultural Revolution were in effect, an estimated fifty million Chinese were sent to labor camps and at least seven million prisoners died.

Starving prisoners were forced to search for food wherever they could find it. They ate snakes, frogs, lizards, worms, and seeds and grains found in animal dung, and resorted to cannibalism. They labored in the fields until they dropped dead from exhaustion and hunger. Tens of thousands died working in lead mines or on construction sites.

Harry Wu, who survived nineteen years in a labor reform camp, called these prisons "a mechanized system for physically, mentally and spiritually crushing human beings." He wrote about his hellish experiences in *Bitter Winds: A Memoir of My Years in China's Gulag*. After emigrating from China to the United States in 1985, he founded the Laogai Research Foundation, a nonprofit organization that compiles factual information about life within the laogai.

Wu explained in an article published in *New Internationalist* that he was able to survive the laogai only "by reducing myself to my most primal state: I became an animal, caring only about satisfying my basic needs. I have heard the same horrible reality echoed in the stories of countless other Laogai survivors. From Mao's time to the current day, the laogai brings its victims to their knees and leaves them to crawl."

Nevertheless, since the mid-1990s, tourists have come to Shaoshan to learn more about Mao. Some still idolize him. As one elderly man explained, "I worship Mao as a god. He didn't just found our nation. He established our system of morality."

Tourists who go to Shaoshan each year may pray before his statue and buy "protection cards" that are said to bear Mao's spirit and to assure safety while traveling. In other parts of the nation, "Mao is revered . . . in much the same way the Virgin Mary is viewed by many Christians as a guardian and protector," according to a report in the *Taipei* (Taiwan) *Times*. "Drivers dangle his picture in their cars, people make incense offerings to his statues in their homes."

TOURISTS IN SHAOSHAN BOW BEFORE A STATUE OF MAO ZEDONG. MANY Chinese make the pilgrimage to Shaoshan each year because they view Mao Zedong as a god.

Although Mao may be a hero to some, especially the elderly and middle-aged, his revolutionary ideas are not commonly promoted across China. The CCP leadership seldom discusses Mao, except for references to Mao Zedong Thought. Many statues of Mao in city squares are gone.

Other indications that Mao has faded as an idol were apparent in 2004 when Maoists were arrested for distributing leaflets titled, "Mao Zedong Forever Our Leader!" The flyer was written to commemorate Mao's death in September and handed out in Zhengzhou, a city that has been called a hotbed of radicals. Two Maoists were charged with "undermining social order and national interests." They were tried and convicted in December and given three-year prison sentences.

Mao's historical contributions to Socialism have also been diminished in some school texts. According to a 2006 report in the *New York Times*, "Socialism has been reduced to a single, short chapter in the senior high school history course" in Shanghai. Mao's name appears only once. Reportedly, the changes in history texts are designed to present "a less violent view" of China's past.

For many current secondary and college-age youth in China, Mao and his revolution are not their most important concerns. Instead, like young people in many parts of the Western world, they are focused on the future and economic opportunities in the years ahead. Yet some Chinese students, even though intent on their economic advancement, still on occasion read Mao's words in the *Little Red Book*. While many of Mao's sayings have no political significance in the New China, some of his teachings are simple truisms for success—such as Mao's instruction to students: "Study hard and make progress every day."

MAO'S MIXED LEGACY

Stuart Schram, a Mao expert and editor of a ten-volume work on Mao's writings, noted both the triumphs and tragedies of Mao's reign. At a 2003 Harvard University conference called "Re-evaluating Mao," Schram pointed out Mao's "faulty judgment" and "vindictiveness." But he also said:

> . . . despite enormous blunders and crimes, [Mao] was a great leader who was trying to do the best for China. I think he'll be remembered for that.

Mao Zedong set the course for China to determine its own destiny. When he took over as leader, he declared that the Chinese had "stood up." With Mao's military strategy and tactics, the country laid the foundation for being free of foreign domination.

In many quarters, Mao is considered a savior of the common people. With his land reform measures, he began the process of overthrowing a system that brutally suppressed peasants. He is given credit for raising the literacy rate, for increasing life expectancy among the masses, for ending child marriages, and for liberating women. Because of his economic and social changes, Mao set the stage for China to emerge from its isolation. The country has gained global economic influence.

On the negative side, Mao was responsible—directly or indirectly—for failed programs and movements such as the Great Leap Forward and the Cultural Revolution, which led to millions of deaths as well as traumatized lives. Also, he has been criticized widely for his contradictory actions. For example, he supported, then

QUOTATIONS FROM CHAIRMAN MAO ZEDONG

Mao's teachings compiled in the *Little Red Book* have been read by people worldwide. Since its publication in the 1960s, about five to six billion copies of the book have been in circulation, in many languages.

The *Little Red Book* contains excerpts from Mao's speeches, reports, manifestos, interviews, and other materials compiled in the five volumes of *Selected Works of Mao Tse-Tung*. Brief quotations cover such subjects as "The Communist Party," "The People's Army," "Political Work," "Self-Reliance and Arduous Struggle," "Cadres," "Youth," "Women," and "Culture and Art." One of the pithiest excerpts included is "Be united, alert, earnest and lively," a motto adopted by a Chinese military college. Another admonishes, "In times of difficulty we must not lose sight of our achievements, must see the bright future and must pluck up our courage."

persecuted colleagues; he condemned Western literature but read it for self-enlightenment; and he praised the simple, peasant life but lived in luxury.

In the 2000s, the CCP avoids responsibility for its role in some of the dark moments of twentieth-century Chinese history. Some scholars who lived through Mao's reign contend that there should be balanced research of the period, looking at the tragedies as well as the triumphs. Whatever credits or demerits Mao receives in the future will depend on whether researchers have free access to documents and can report without bias the details of the twenty-seven years of Mao's dictatorship.

WHO'S WHO?

CHIANG KAI-SHEK (1887–1975) Born in Zhejiang Province, Chiang trained for the military in Japan and Russia. He was a military aide to Sun Yat-sen, leader of the Kuomintang (KMT), or Nationalist Party. After Sun's death, he led an expedition to oust warlords controlling much of northern China. He became the leader of the Nationalist government in 1928. During his career, he formed an alliance with the Communists and then turned against them, launching a long civil war. His forces also took part in a war with Japan (1937–1945), which overlapped with World War II. After the Japanese were expelled in 1945, civil war erupted again between the Communists and the KMT. The Communists won control of the country in 1949, and Chiang was forced to flee to Taiwan, where he established a Nationalist government with himself in firm control as president. He ruled as a dictator until his death in 1975.

DENG XIAOPING (1904–1997) A respected Communist leader, Deng Xiaoping helped bring about economic and political reforms after Mao Zedong's failed Great Leap Forward and Cultural Revolution. Deng was born into a fairly wealthy family in Sichuan Province. He studied in France and became a Marxist and political activist in that country and also in Moscow. When he returned to China, he became a Communist Party organizer and began his lifelong service to the party. He helped lead the Red Army on the Long March and became one of Mao's trusted lieutenants. He was purged from the party as a "capitalist roader" during the Cultural Revolution, but Mao brought him back in 1973 as vice premier. He was purged again by the Gang of Four in 1976 and, after being "rehabilitated," began policies to modernize China, efforts that continued until his death in 1997. His reformist reputation was tainted by his decision to use PLA troops to violently suppress student demonstrators gathered in Tiananmen Square in 1989.

HE ZIZHEN (1910–1984) The daughter of a landlord, He Zizhen became a Communist organizer during her late teenage years. She met Mao when she was eighteen years old and lived with him for two years before they were married in 1930. Eventually they are believed to have had six children—their first child, a daughter, died, as did their last, who lived only six months. At least two children were abandoned. On the Long March (1934–1935), He Zizhen accompanied Mao, leaving their two-year old son behind. She was pregnant at the time and another daughter was born while she was on the trek. She was forced to leave the baby in the care of a peasant woman and never saw the child again. In 1937 Mao sent He Zizhen to the Soviet Union for psychiatric treatment. While she was gone, Mao met well-known film actress Jiang Qing, or Chiang Ch'ing, and though he did not formally divorce He, he married Jiang in 1939. He Zizhen died in 1984.

JIANG QING (1914–1991) Different historical accounts give varied years for Jiang's birth, ranging from 1912 to 1914. She was born in Shandong Province and received very little education until she enrolled in a drama school in 1928. She worked in the film industry during the 1930s and used the stage name Lan Ping. In 1938 she joined the Communist Party and traveled to Yenan, the Communist headquarters, where she met Mao. The two were married in 1939.

Jiang was not in the spotlight, except for her role as Mao's hostess, until the Cultural Revolution (1966–1969). She was appointed the deputy director of the Cultural Group within the CCP's Executive Committee. She began a cultural reform movement that included banning traditional opera and ballet and allowing only performances with revolutionary themes. The "reforms" also became attacks on leading Chinese artists, writers, and intellectuals. With Mao's support, she and three other top Communists, known as the Gang of Four, incited Red Guards to denounce and brutalize those who did not follow the revolutionary line. After Mao's death, the Gang of Four was arrested, Jiang included. She was imprisoned until 1991. Some sources declare she died in prison, and others say she committed suicide shortly after her release.

LIN BIAO (CA. 1907–1971) Born in Hubei Province, Lin Biao was eighteen when he entered an officers' training school at the Whampoa Military Academy in Canton. He became known as a brilliant military hero by the time he was twenty-eight years old and took part in Chiang Kai-shek's Nationalist expedition to oust warlords in northern China. When Chiang turned on the Communists, Lin joined Mao Zedong's Red Army. He led guerrilla troops against the Nationalists and is said to have been victorious in every battle. He was Mao's trusted commander, became minister of defense, and was responsible for compiling some of Mao's writings in *Quotations of Chairman Mao*, popularly called the *Little Red Book*.

Mao designated Lin as his successor. But as Lin gained political power, he apparently became a threat to Mao. According to the CCP's official assessment, Lin planned to assassinate the chairman, the plot was uncovered, and Lin fled with family members by plane to Russia in 1971. The plane crashed, killing all on board. Yet there is no certainty about Lin's disappearance. Some historians suspect he could have been executed.

RICHARD M. NIXON (1913–1994) In 1969 Richard Nixon became the thirty-seventh president of the United States. He began his term with hopes to end the war in Vietnam quickly and to ease the rivalry between China and Russia and reduce the threat of war with the two Communist countries. The Vietnam conflict continued for four more years before U.S. troops were withdrawn, but Nixon achieved notable accomplishments in his quest for a more stable balance of power. During his visits to Beijing and Moscow in 1972, he reduced tensions with China and the Soviet Union. He held frank talks with Mao Zedong and Zhou Enlai. In a document called the Shanghai Communiqué, both the United States and China agreed to respect each other's sovereignty and territorial integrity, to peaceful coexistence, and to increased trade.

Nixon's foreign affairs achievements were overshadowed in his second term when his administration became involved in a break-in at the headquarters of the Democratic National Committee in the Watergate building. The Republican Committee to Re-elect the President was held responsible, and some officials were forced to resign and were later convicted of covering up the offense. Nixon declared he was not involved, but his own tape recordings proved otherwise. In 1974 he faced impeachment and became the first U.S. president to resign from office.

SUN YAT-SEN (1866–1925) He has been called the Father of the Chinese Nation, although much of his life was spent outside China. Sun was educated in Honolulu, where he was influenced by Christianity and Western ideas. He received a medical degree in Hong Kong and practiced medicine for a short time. But his central passion was the overthrow of the Manchus—the Qing dynasty. He was convinced that China had to become a republic, modernize its agricultural practices, and industrialize, or else remain a backward country. To achieve these goals, Sun became a revolutionary and toured Europe and the United States to raise funds for his cause.

Several times Sun attempted to stir up revolution against the Manchus, but the uprisings failed. When a revolution ousted the Qing dynasty in 1912, Sun was in the United States but returned to China to establish the Kuomintang (KMT)—the Nationalist Party. The KMT army was organized to rid the country of warlords and unify the nation under a Soviet-type Communism. Sun sent his military aide, Chiang Kai-shek, to Moscow to study the Soviet military and political systems. Sun Yat-sen died in 1925, and the following year, Chiang led Nationalist and Communist troops, called the United Forces, against China's warlords.

YANG KAIHUI (1901–1930) She was the daughter of Mao Zedong's respected teacher Yang Changji and was born in Hunan Province. Mao often visited the Yang home and ate meals with the family. Yang Kaihui and Mao fell in love, and they married in 1920. But Mao was soon unfaithful, having sexual liaisons with several women. While Yang was devastated, she always forgave Mao. The couple had three sons, Anying, Anqing, and Anlong. The youngest, Anlong, died when he was four years old.

Although Yang Kaihui joined the Communist Party in 1921, she became disillusioned, especially after Mao left with a Red Army force to fight the Nationalists. He divorced Yang in 1927. She stayed in Changsha, her family home, with their children. In 1930 Mao attacked Changsha, which was ruled by a Nationalist general. Even though Yang was not involved with Communist activities, the Nationalists took revenge by arresting Yang and Anying, the eldest son. The Nationalists told her they would spare her life if she denounced Mao. She refused to do so and was executed in November 1930.

TZU HSI (1835–1908) Tzu Hsi was the daughter of a Manchu official who died during her childhood. She became the concubine of Emperor Hsien Feng and gave birth to the emperor's only son, T'sai Ch'un. When Hsien Feng died in 1861, the five-year-old T'sai Ch'un was named emperor. Tzu Hsi and Hsien's wife Tzu An became co-regents, governing China in place of the minor ruler. The two empress dowagers ruled until T'ung-chih came of age in 1873, but he died two years later. Tzu Hsi then had the power to choose a new emperor—her three-year-old nephew, Kuang Hsu. When her nephew's mother and the co-regent Tzu An died soon afterward, Tzu Hsi gained complete control.

Tzu Hsi's rule has been described as ruthless, corrupt, and tyrannical. When Emperor Kuang Hsu was able to rule, he attempted to initiate reforms to modernize China, but that infuriated Tzu Hsi. She had Kuang Hsu imprisoned on an island and overturned all reform rulings. Eventually because of the failed Boxer Rebellion against foreigners in China, she had to change her policies and allow construction of railroads, ban opium trading, and pledge to set up a representative government. She became seriously ill in 1908 and knew she was dying. Before she died in November of that year, she declared another nephew, three-year-old P'u Yi, emperor. He was overthrown during the Nationalist revolution.

YUAN SHIKAI (1859–1916) A major figure in China, Yuan Shikai was a military official in the Manchu dynasty and supported the Empress Dowager Tzu Hsi against the reform movement of Emperor Kuang Hsu. Yuan suppressed the Boxer Rebellion, the antiforeign movement in

China. After Tzu died, Yuan was forced to retire, but when the 1911 revolution began, the dynasty asked him to return to command the army. In exchange, he was promised the premiership.

When the Manchu relinquished the throne, Yuan became the first president of the Chinese Republic, with headquarters in Peking (Beijing). At the same time, Sun Yat-sen had set up a provisional republic based on his ideas in Nanjing (Nanking) on the Yangtze River. To avoid a civil war, Sun agreed to allow Yuan to head the government.

Yuan steadily gained control and created a government made up of his cronies. On the threat of war with Japan, he capitulated to Japanese demands to control much of China. Revolts erupted and Yuan's power diminished. He died in 1916.

ZHOU ENLAI (1898–1976) Zhou Enlai was one of China's most respected leaders. As a youth, he took part in the May Fourth Movement and was imprisoned for his activism. After several months, he was released and went to France with a work-study group. While there he joined the Communist Party in 1922 and set up several European branches of the CCP. Zhou returned to China in 1924 and joined Sun Yat-sen's Kuomintang (KMT), or Nationalists, who had formed an alliance with the Communists. He was appointed deputy director of the political department of the Whampoa Military Academy, headed by Chiang Kai-shek. When Sun Yat-sen died in 1925, Chiang became the KMT leader and broke the alliance with the Communists, purging and killing many of them.

Zhou escaped, joining Mao and the Red Army in the Long March (1934–1935) to northwest China, where a Communist stronghold was set up. After the establishment of the People's Republic of China in 1949, Zhou became prime minister and foreign minister. He gave up the foreign ministry in 1958 but kept the premiership throughout Mao's reign and the chaos of the Great Leap Forward and the Red Guard attacks during the Cultural Revolution. After Zhou's death in 1976, thousands of Chinese gathered at Tiananmen Square on Qingming, a traditional festival for remembering the dead, to honor Zhou as a hero.

TIMELINE

1644–1911 The Qing, China's last dynasty, reigns.

1893 Mao Zedong is born in Hunan Province, China.

1895 Sun Yat-sen begins to organize an anti-Qing group.

1911 The Qing dynasty is overthrown, and a republic is established.

1919 The May Fourth Movement spawns numerous protests and demonstrations against the Western decision to give German territories in China to the Japanese.

1920 Mao marries Yang Kaihui.

1921 Mao attends the First Congress of the Chinese Communist Party.

1923 The Chinese Nationalist Party Kuomintang (KMT) and Chinese Communist Party create the United Front against Japanese aggressors.

1925 Sun dies, and Chiang Kai-shek becomes leader of the KMT.

1926 Chiang, with aid from Communists, begins Northern Expedition to rout warlords and reunify China.

1927 Chiang turns on Communists, killing many. Mao flees to the mountains and helps form the Red Army.

1934-1935 The Long March takes place. Communists trek to northwest China and establish a new headquarters in Yenan.

1937 Chiang is kidnapped and released. KMT and Communists form a national United Front against the Japanese.

1937–1945 The second Sino-Japanese War takes place.

1949 The People's Republic of China is proclaimed.

1950–1953 The Korean War is fought, with U.S.-led United Nations and South Korean forces fighting against Chinese- and Soviet-backed North Korean forces.

1956 The Hundred Flowers Campaign begins, urging people to criticize the Chinese Communist Party.

1957 An Anti-Rightist Campaign persecutes those who speak up against the CCP.

1958–1960 The Great Leap Forward campaign results in millions of deaths.

1966 The Great Proletarian Cultural Revolution begins.

1972 U.S. president Richard Nixon visits China.

1976 Mao Zedong dies on September 9.

1977–PRESENT Mao's legacy is debated in China and the rest of the world.

GLOSSARY

capitalism: an economic system based on private ownership of property, resources, and the means to produce and distribute goods

Communism: an economic system in which there is public ownership and government control of resources and the means needed to produce and distribute goods

dynasties: a series of kings or emperors from the same family who pass their right to rule from one member to another

empress dowager: a title given to the mother of a Chinese emperor or the widow of an emperor

garrison: a military post

guerrilla tactics: a nontraditional form of battle with small units that make swift surprise attacks

laogai: a Chinese word meaning "reform through labor" and the term for Chinese prison camps

League of Nations: an international organization created after World War I to help prevent future wars and to pursue world peace. Neither China nor the United States joined the short-lived organization.

Manchus: non-Chinese people whose original homeland was Manchuria

manifesto: a written declaration of a person's or group's intent, beliefs, or principles

Marxists: people who believe in the economic, social, and political theories of nineteenth-century philosopher Karl Marx

militia: armed citizens, rather than professional soldiers, who make up a military force

nationalism: a belief that a nation should be self-ruled, as opposed to ruled by outside powers

Qingming: a traditional Chinese festival for remembering the dead

Red Army: Communist armed forces

Red Guards: radical Chinese youths who espoused Maoist ideas and attacked those considered to be anti-Mao

regent: a person who governs in place of an absent, disabled, or minor king or other ruler. A co-regent is a person who governs along with another regent.

Tiananmen: the main gate or entrance to the Imperial Palace Grounds, commonly called the Forbidden City, in Beijing, China

warlord: a military leader with control over a region

SELECTED BIBLIOGRAPHY

Becker, Jasper. *Hungry Ghosts: Mao's Secret Famine*. New York: Free Press, 1996.

Bernstein, Richard. "A Leader's Rise, a Widow's Fall." *Time*. January 12, 1981. http://www.time.com/time/magazine/article/0,9171,922352,00.html (October 21, 2006).

British Broadcasting Company. "China Marks Tangshan Earthquake." *BBC*. July 28, 2006. http://news.bbc.co.uk/2/hi/asia-pacific/5221296.stm (October 21, 2006).

Chen, Da. *China's Son: Growing Up in the Cultural Revolution*. New York: Delacorte Press, 2001.

China.org. "Ping Pong Diplomacy." *china.org.cn*. July 8, 2004. http://www.china.org.cn/english/features/olympics/100660.htm (October 21, 2006).

Columbia University. "The Commune System." *Columbia University, East Asian Curriculum Project*. July 25, 2005. http://afe.easia.columbia.edu/china/gov/communes.htm (October 21, 2006).

"Defying Death (Jiang Qing, Chairman Mao's Wife)." *Time*. February 7, 1983, 38.

Deng Xiaoping. "Build Socialism with Chinese Characteristics." Excerpt from a talk with the Japanese delegation to the second session of the Council of Sino-Japanese Non-Governmental Persons. June 30, 1984. http://www.wellesley.edu/Polisci/wj/China/Deng/Building.htm (October 21, 2006).

Duffy, Michael, ed. "Primary Documents: 'Twenty-One Demands' Made by Japan to China, 18 January 1915." *First World War.com*. September 29, 2002. http://www.firstworldwar.com/source/21demands.htm (October 21, 2006).

Durdin, Frank Tillman. "All Captives Slain." *New York Times*. December 18, 1937. Paul Halsall. In "Modern History Sourcebook: The Nanking Massacre, 1937." August 1997. http://www.fordham.edu/halsall/mod/nanking.html (October 21, 2006).

Ebrey, Patricia Buckley. *The Cambridge Illustrated History of China*. New York: Cambridge University Press, 1996.

Epoch Times. "Nine Commentaries on the Communist Party." January 12, 2005. http://www10.epochtimes.com/9pingdownload/English/9ping_en.pdf (October 21, 2006).

Gale, Fred. "China's Statistics: Are They Reliable?" *China's Food and Agriculture: Issues for the 21st Century*. April 1, 2002. Washington, DC: United States Department of Agriculture Economic Research Service. http://www.ers.usda.gov/publications/aib775/ (October 21, 2006).

Gewertz, Ken. "Mao Under a Microscope." *Harvard University Gazette*. December 11, 2003. http://www.news.harvard.edu/gazette/2003/12.11/23-mao.html (October 23, 2006).

Gittings, John. *The Changing Face of China from Mao to Market*. Oxford: Oxford University Press, 2005.

Guillermaz, Jacques. *A History of the Chinese Communist Party 1921–1949*. Translated by Anne Destenay. New York: Random House, 1972.

Harms, William. "China's Great Leap Forward." *University of Chicago Chronicle*. March 14, 1996. http://chronicle.uchicago.edu/960314/china.shtml (October 21, 2006).

Harris, Nigel. "The Workers and Peasants in the People's Republic." Part III. *The Mandate of Heaven*. July 26, 2001. http://www.marxists.de/china/harris/10-peasants.htm (July 15, 2006).

Hore, Charlie. "It Is Right to Rebel." *Socialist Review*. March 1994. http://pubs.socialistreviewindex.org.uk/sr173/hore.htm (October 21, 2006).

Jiang, Ji-Li. *Red Scarf Girl: A Memoir of the Cultural Revolution.* New York: HarperCollins, 1997.

Jung Chang. *Wild Swans: Three Daughters of China.* New York: Anchor / Doubleday, 1991.

Jung Chang, and Jon Halliday. *Mao: The Unknown Story.* New York: Alfred A. Knopf, 2005.

Kahn, Joseph. "Where's Mao? Chinese Revise History Books." *New York Times.* September 1, 2006.

Kissinger, Henry A. "Memorandum for the President." *George Washington University.* July 14, 1971. http://www.gwu.edu/~nsarchiv/NSAEBB/ NSAEBB66/ch-40.pdf (October 21, 2006).

Li Changyu, "Mao's 'Killing Quotas.'" *China Rights Forum.* 2005. http://hrichina.org/public/PDFs/CRF.4.2005/CRF-2005-4_Quota.pdf. (April 16, 2007).

Li Zhisui. *The Private Life of Chairman Mao: The Memoirs of Mao's Personal Physician.* Translated by Tai Hung-chao. New York: Random House, 1994.

Long Bow Group. "Chairman Mao's Mausoleum." *Morning Sun.* N.d. http://www.morningsun.org/stages/tsquare/mausoleum.html (October 21, 2006).

Mack, Joseph. "The Cultural Revolution—The 'Bloody' Sixties." *Epoch Times.* May 17, 2006. http://www.theepochtimes.com/news/ 6-5-17/41619.html (October 21, 2006).

Malaspina, Ann. *The Chinese Revolution and Mao Zedong in World History.* Berkeley Heights, NJ: Enslow Publishers, 2004.

Mao Tse-Tung. *Mao Tse-Tung Selected Works.* Vols. 1–5. New York: International Publishers, 1954.

Mao Zedong. *Mao Tse-Tung on Guerrilla Warfare.* Translated by Samuel B. Griffith. New York: Praeger Publishers, 1961.

——. "Mao Zedong: A Long Life Comes to an End." *Morning Sun.* N.d. http://www.morningsun.org/living/dying/mao_end.html (October 21, 2006).

——. *Quotations from Chairman Mao Tse-tung.* Peking: Foreign Languages Press, 1976.

Marcy, Sam. "Jiang Qing and the Cultural Revolution." *Workers World.* June 30, 1991. http://www.workers.org/marcy/1991/sm910620.html (October 21, 2006).

Mo Bo. "I Was a Teenage Red Guard." *New Internationalist.* April 1987. http://www.newint.org/issue170/teenage.htm (October 21, 2006).

Monthly Review. "On December 24, 2004, Maoists in China Get Three Year Prison Sentences for Leafleting." January 2005. http://www .monthlyreview.org/0105commentary.htm (October 21, 2006).

Moraes, Frank. *Report on Mao's China.* New York: Macmillan Company, 1954.

Muhlhahn, Klaus. "'Remembering a Bitter Past': The Trauma of China's Labor Camps, 1949–1978." *History and Memory: Studies in Representation of the Past.* Fall–Winter 2004: 108-139.

New York Times. "Obituary: Text of the Announcement Issued by Peking Reporting Death of Chairman Mao." September 10, 1976. http://www.nytimes.com/learning/general/onthisday/bday/ 1226a.html (October 21, 2006).

Peking Review. "Red Guards Destroy the Old and Establish the New." September 2, 1966. http://www.morningsun.org/smash/pr9_1966 .html (October 21, 2006).

Pelissier, Roger. *The Awakening of China 1793–1949.* Edited and translated by Martin Kieffer. New York: G. P. Putnam's Sons, 1967.

People's Daily Online. "A 15-year-old American Girl and Ping Pong Diplomacy." November 14, 2003. http://english.people.com.cn/ 200311/14/eng20031114_128247.shtml (October 21, 2006).

———. "We Can Develop a Market Economy Under Socialism." *Deng Xiaoping's Talk with Economic Experts.* November 26, 1979. http://english.people.com.cn/dengxp/vol2/text/b1370.html (October 21, 2006).

Qui Jin. "Distorting History: Lessons from the Lin Biao Incident." *Old Dominion University's Quest.* June 2002. http://www.odu.edu/ao/ instadv/quest/linbiao.html (October 21, 2006).

Schram, Stuart. *Political Leaders of the Twentieth Century: Mao Tse-Tung.* Harmondsworth, UK: Penguin Books, 1972.

———. *The Political Thought of Mao Tse Tung.* Rev. ed. New York: Frederick A. Praeger Publishers, 1969.

Shawki, Ahmed. "China: From Mao to Deng." *International Socialist Review.* Summer 1997. http://www.isreview.org/issues/01/mao_to _deng_1.shtml (October 21, 2006).

Short, Philip. *Mao: A Life.* New York: Henry Holt, 2000.

Smith, Bill. "Mao Loses Ideological Might but Remains Popular Icon." *Deutsche Presse Agentur.* September 4, 2006. http://rawstory.com/ news/2006/Mao_loses_ideological_might_but_rem_09042006.html (October 21, 2006).

Snow, Edgar. *Red Star over China.* Rev. ed. New York: Grove Press, 1968.

Society for Anglo-Chinese Understanding. "A Boy's Experience of the Cultural Revolution in the Countryside." *SACU.* 2001. http://sacu.org/cutp.html (October 21, 2006).

———. "Decline and Fall of Lin Biao." *SACU.* March 1973. http://www .sacu.org/linbiao.html (October 21, 2006).

Spence, Jonathan D. *The Gate of Heavenly Peace: The Chinese and Their Revolution 1895–1980.* New York: The Viking Press, 1981.

———. *Mao Zedong.* New York: Penguin Group, 2006.

Taipei Times. "Mao Zedong Joins the Pantheon of China's Folk Gods." September 6, 2006. http://www.taipeitimes.com/News/world/archives/2006/09/06/2003326405 (October 21, 2006).

Tang, Rose. "Revolution's Children: The Collapse of Ideology Leaves Generations Adrift in a Moral Vacuum." *Asiaweek.* September 24, 1999. http://www.pathfinder.com/asiaweek/magazine/99/0924/cn_journeys.html#artist (October 21, 2006).

Time. "Dance of the Scorpion." January 13, 1967. http://www.time.com/time/magazine/article/0,9171,843231,00.html (October 21, 2006).

Time Editors. *Great People of the 20th Century.* New York: Time Books, 1996.

Trueman, Chris. "The Great Leap Forward." *History Learning Site.* 2000. http://www.historylearningsite.co.uk/great_leap_forward.htm (October 21, 2006).

U.S. Department of State's Bureau of International Information Programs. "Joint Communique of the United States of America and the People's Republic of China." *USINFO.state.gov.* February 28, 1972. http://usinfo.state.gov/eap/Archive_Index/joint_communique_1972.html (October 21, 2006).

Watts, Jonathan. "Mao Returns to Haunt and Comfort His People." *Guardian.* December 27, 2003. http://www.longmarchspace.com/media/guardian%20unlimiter.htm (October 21, 2006).

Wheeler, W. Reginald. *China and the World War.* Chapter 1. New York: The Macmillan Company, 1919. http://www.lib.byu.edu/~rdh/wwi/comment/chinawwi/ChinaC1.htm (October 21, 2006).

Wingfield-Hayes, Rupert. "Mao: Powerful Symbol, Abandoned Ideals." *British Broadcasting Company.* September 10, 2001. http://news.bbc .co.uk/2/hi/asia-pacific/1535300.stm (October 21, 2006).

Worden, Robert L., Andrea Matles Savada, and Ronald E. Dolan, eds. "The Ninth National Party Congress to the Demise of Lin Biao, 1969–71." In *China: A Country Study.* Washington, DC: Federal Research Division of the Library of Congress. July 1987. http://www.country-data .com/cgi-bin/query/r-2607.html (October 21, 2006).

Wu, Harry, and Carolyn Wakeman. *Bitter Winds: A Memoir of My Years in China's Gulag.* New York: John Wiley & Sons, 1994.

SOURCE NOTES

6 Roger Pelissier, *The Awakening of China 1793–1949,* edited and translated by Martin Kieffer (New York: G. P. Putnam's Sons, 1967), 501–503.

8 Mao Tse-Tung, "The Chinese People Have Stood Up!" September 21, 1949, in *Selected Works of Mao Tse-Tung,* Vol. 5, 2004, http://www.marxists.org/reference/archive/mao/selected-works/volume-5/index.htm (February 28, 2007).

8–9 Rose Tang, "Revolution's Children: The Collapse of Ideology Leaves Generations Adrift in a Moral Vacuum," *Asiaweek,* September 24, 1999, http://www.pathfinder.com/asiaweek/magazine/99/0924/cn_journeys.html#artist (February 28, 2007).

14 Edgar Snow, *Red Star over China,* rev. ed. (New York: Grove Press, 1968), 131.

14 Ibid.

16 J. Buschini, "The Boxer Rebellion," 2000, http://www.smplanet.com/imperialism/fists.html (October 23, 2006).

17 Snow, *Red Star over China,* 147.

17 Jonathan Spence, *Mao Zedong* (New York: Penguin Group, 2006), 11.

18 Snow, *Red Star over China,* 140–141.

18 Ibid., 142.

19 Ibid.

21 W. Reginald Wheeler, *China and the World War,* Chapter 1 (New York: Macmillan Company, 1919), http://www.lib.byu.edu/~rdh/wwi/comment/chinawwi/ChinaC1.htm (October 21, 2006).

21 Michael Duffy, ed., "Primary Documents: 'Twenty-One Demands' Made by Japan to China, 18 January 1915," *First World War.com.*, September 29, 2002, http://www.firstworldwar.com/source/21demands.htm (October 21, 2006).

23 Pelissier, *The Awakening of China 1793–1949,* 274.

23 Ibid.

24–25 Mao Zedong, "Toward a New Golden Age," July 1919, in Stuart R. Schram, *The Political Thought of Mao Tse Tung,* rev. ed. (New York: Frederick A. Praeger Publishers, 1969), 162–163.

25 Mao Zedong, *Selected Works of Mao Tse-Tung,* Maoist Documentation Project, 2004, http://www.marxists.org/reference/archive/mao/selected-works/volume-6/mswv6_03.htm (October 23, 2006).

25 Mao Zedong, *Selected Works of Mao Tse-Tung,* n.d., http://www.marxists.org/reference/archive/mao/selected-works/volume-6/mswv6_04.htm (May 9, 2007).

26 Snow, *Red Star over China,* 155.

26 Ibid.

28 Spence, *Mao Zedong,* 52.

28 Stuart Schram, *Political Leaders of the Twentieth Century: Mao Tse-Tung* (Harmondsworth, UK: Penguin Books, 1972), 65.

28 Snow, *Red Star over China,* 158.

28 Ibid.

33 Mao Tse-Tung, *Mao Tse-Tung Selected Works* (New York: International Publishers, 1954), 1:25.

33 Ibid., 18.

33 Ibid., 22.

33 Ibid., 27.

35 Mao Tse-Tung, "On the Reissue of the Three Main Rules of Discipline and the Eight Points for Attention-Instruction of the General Headquarters of the Chinese People's Liberation Army," October 10, 1947, in *Selected Works of Mao Tse-Tung* (New York, International Publishers, n.d.), 5:155.

36 Snow, *Red Star over China,* 174.

36–37 Mao Tse-Tung, *Mao Tse-Tung Selected Works,* 1:82–83.

38 Ibid., 106.

38 Snow, *Red Star over China,* 180.

40 Spence, *Mao Zedong,* 87.

40 Mao Tse-Tung, *Mao Tse-Tung Selected Works,* 2:272–273.

45 Frank Tillman Durdin, "All Captives Slain," *New York Times,* December 18, 1937, in Paul Halsall, "Modern History Sourcebook: The Nanking Massacre, 1937" August 1997, 1, 10, http://www.fordham.edu/ halsall/mod/nanking.html (October 21, 2006).

47 Mao Zedong, "The Chinese People Have Stood Up!" September 21, 1949, *UCLA Center for East Asian Studies, East Asian Studies Documents,* http://www.isop.ucla .edu/eas/documents/ mao490921.htm (October 23, 2006).

48 Ibid.

50 Mao Tse-Tung, "In Commemoration of the 28th Anniversary of the Communist Party of China," speech, June 30, 1949, in *Mao Tse-Tung Selected Works,* 5:411.

51 Ibid., 423.

51–52 Ibid., 417–418.

54 Mao Zedong, "Order to the Chinese People's Volunteers," excerpts from an order issued by

Comrade Mao Tsetung to the Chinese People's Volunteers, October 1950, *marxists.org*, 2004, http://www.marxists.org/ reference/archive/mao/ selected-works/volume -5/mswv5_10.htm (October 23, 2006).

55 Patricia Buckley Ebrey, *The Cambridge Illustrated History of China* (New York: Cambridge University Press, 1996), 297.

56 Li Changyu, "Mao's 'Killing Quotas,'" *China Rights Forum*, No. 4, 2005, http://hrichina.org/fs/ view/downloadables/ pdf/crf/CRF-2005-4 _Quota.pdf (October 21, 2006).

57 Chen Han-seng, "The First 5-Year Plan: What It Means," *China Today*, October 1955, http://www.chinatoday.co m.cn/English/20021/1950 nian.htm (October 21, 2006).

58 Ibid.

58 Robert L. Worden, Andrea Matles Savada, and Ronald E. Dolan, eds., "The First Five-Year Plan, 1953–57," In *China: A Country Study*. Washington, DC: Federal Research Division of the Library of Congress, July 1987. http:// countrystudies.us/china/ 87.htm (February 25, 2007).

60 Frank Moraes, *Report on Mao's China* (New York: Macmillan Company, 1954), 130.

61 Quoted in Li Zhisui, Tai Hung-chao, trans., *The Private Life of Chairman Mao: The Memoirs of Mao's Personal Physician*. (New York: Random House, 1994), 201.

61 Vivien Pik-Kwan Chan, "Survivor Unbowed after Persecution," *South China Morning Post*, June 29, 2001, http://special.scmp .com/commpartyat80/ profiles/ZZZYEZUBEOC .html (October 21, 2006).

62 Mao Zedong, "The Masses Can Do Anything," *Selected Works of Mao Tse-Tung,* September 28, 1958, http://www.marxists.org/reference/archive/mao/selected-works/volume-8/mswv8_16.htm (October 21, 2006).

64–65 Jung Chang, *Wild Swans: Three Daughters of China* (New York: Anchor Books / Doubleday, 1991), 220.

68 Ahmed Shawki, "China: From Mao to Deng," *International Socialist Review,* Summer 1997, http://www.isreview.org/issues/01/mao_to_deng_1.shtml (October 21, 2006).

68 Jung Chang and Jon Halliday, *Mao: The Unknown Story* (New York: Alfred A. Knopf, 2005), 460.

68 Jasper Becker, *Hungry Ghosts: Mao's Secret Famine* (New York: Free Press, 1996), 292.

68 Ibid., xii.

69 William Harms, "China's Great Leap Forward," University of Chicago Chronicle, March 14, 1996, http://chronicle.uchicago.edu/960314/china.shtml (October 21, 2006).

71 Shawki, "China: From Mao to Deng."

73 Mo Bo, "I Was a Teenage Red Guard," *New Internationalist,* April 1987, http://www.newint.org/issue170/teenage.htm (October 21, 2006).

74 *Peking Review,* "Red Guards Destroy the Old and Establish the New," September 2, 1966, 17, http://www.morningsun.org/smash/pr9_1966.html (October 21, 2006).

75 Ji-Li Jiang, *Red Scarf Girl: A Memoir of the Cultural Revolution* (New York: HarperCollins, 1997), 256, 260–261.

76 Mo Bo, "I Was a Teenage Red Guard."

76 Joseph Mack, "The Cultural Revolution—The 'Bloody' Sixties," *Epoch Times,* May 17, 2006, http://www .theepochtimes.com/ news/6-5-17/41619.html (October 21, 2006).

81 Society for Anglo-Chinese Understanding, "A Boy's Experience of the Cultural Revolution in the Countryside," *SACU,* 2001, http://sacu.org/ cutp.html (October 21, 2006).

81 Spence, *Mao Zedong,* 171.

82 Liang Heng and Judith Shapiro, *Son of the Revolution* (New York: Vintage Books / Random House, 1984), 46.

83 Philip Short, *Mao: A Life* (New York: Henry Holt, 2000), 550–551.

83 Li, *The Private Life of Chairman Mao,* 86.

83 Mao Tse-Tung, "Report of an Investigation into the Peasant Movement in Hunan," March 1927, in *Mao Tse-Tung Selected Works,* 1:38.

84 Mao Tse-Tung, "Essential Points in Land Reform in the New Liberated Areas," February 15, 1948, in *Mao Tse-Tung Selected Works,* 5:202.

85 Jung Chang, *Wild Swans: Three Daughters of China,* 167.

85 Ibid.

85 Ibid.

86–87 Moraes, *Report on Mao's China,* 101, 103.

87 Ibid., 109.

89 Spence, *Mao Zedong,* 173.

90 China.org, "Ping Pong Diplomacy," *china.org.cn,* July 8, 2004, http://www.china.org.cn/ english/features/ olympics/100660.htm (October 21, 2006).

90 *People's Daily Online,* "A 15-year-old American Girl and Ping Pong Diplomacy," November 14, 2003, http://english .peopledaily.com.cn/ 200311/14/eng20031114 _128247.shtml (October 21, 2006).

90 Ibid.

90 Ibid.

92 Short, *Mao: A Life,* 601.

92 Ibid, 602.

93 Henry A. Kissinger, "Memorandum for the President," *George Washington University,* July 14, 1971, http://www.gwu.edu/ ~nsarchiv/NSAEBB/ NSAEBB66/ch-40.pdf (October 21, 2006).

93 Henry Kissinger, *White House Years* (Little, Brown and Co., 1979), 1054.

95 U.S. Department of State's Bureau of International Information Programs, "Joint Communique of the United States of America and the People's Republic of China," *USINFO.state .gov.,* February 28, 1972, http://usinfo.state.gov/ea p/Archive_Index/joint _communique_1972.html (October 21, 2006).

96–97 Worden, Savada, and Dolan. "The Ninth National Party Congress to the Demise of Lin Biao, 1969–71."

98 Society for Anglo-Chinese Understanding, "Decline and Fall of Lin Biao," *SACU,* March 1973, 3, http://www.sacu .org/linbiao.html (October 21, 2006).

98–99 Qui Jin, "Distorting History: Lessons from the Lin Biao Incident," *Old Dominion University's Quest,* June 2002, http:// www.odu.edu/ao/ instadv/quest/linbiao.htm l (October 21, 2006).

99 Ibid.

99 Ibid.

100 Short, *Mao: A Life,* 616.

100 Spence, *Mao Zedong,* 174.

100–101 Sam Marcy, "Jiang Qing and the Cultural Revolution," *Workers World,* June 30, 1991, http://www.workers.org/ marcy/1991/sm910620 .html (October 21, 2006).

101 Snow, *Red Star over China,* 460.

102 Short, *Mao: A Life,* 620.

102–103 Ibid., 623.

103 Jung Chang, *Wild Swans: Three Daughters of China,* 491.

102 Ibid.

105 Ibid, 493.

105 Ibid.

106 Li Zhisui, *The Private Life of Chairman Mao,* 260.

109 Short, *Mao: A Life,* 621.

109 Li Zhisui, *The Private Life of Chairman Mao,* 624.

109–110 *New York Times,* "Obituary: Text of the Announcement Issued by Peking Reporting Death of Chairman Mao," September 10, 1976, http://www.nytimes .com/learning/general/ onthisday/bday/1226a .html (October 21, 2006).

110–111 Long Bow Group, Mao Zedong: A Long Life Comes to an End," *Morning Sun,* n.d., http://www.morningsun .org/living/dying/mao _end.html (October 21, 2006).

111 Long Bow Group, "Chairman Mao's Mausoleum," *Morning Sun,* n.d., http://www .morningsun.org/stages/ tsquare/mausoleum.html (October 21, 2006).

111 Rupert Wingfield-Hayes, "Mao: Powerful Symbol, Abandoned Ideals," *British Broadcasting Company,* September 10, 2001, http://news.bbc.co.uk/2/ hi/asia-pacific/1535300 .stm (October 21, 2006).

113 Li Zhisui, *The Private Life of Chairman Mao,* 20.

114 John Gittings, *The Changing Face of China: From Mao to Market* (Oxford: Oxford University Press, 2005), 164.

115 Jung Chang, *Wild Swans: Three Daughters of China*, 496.

117 People's Daily Online, "We Can Develop a Market Economy under Socialism," Deng Xiaoping's Talk with Economic Experts, November 26, 1979, http://english.people .com.cn/dengxp/vol2/ text/b1370.html (October 21, 2006).

118 Deng Xiaoping, "Build Socialism with Chinese Characteristics," Excerpt from a talk with the Japanese delegation to the second session of the Council of Sino-Japanese Non-Governmental Persons. June 30, 1984, http://www.wellesley.edu/ Polisci/wj/China/Deng/ Building.htm (October 21, 2006).

118 Ibid.

118 Ibid.

118 Richard Bernstein, "A Leader's Rise, a Widow's Fall," *Time*, January 12, 1981, http://www.time .com/time/magazine/ article/0,9171,922352,00 .html (October 21, 2006).

119 Ibid.

119 *Time*, "Defying Death," February 7, 1983, 38.

121 Harry Wu, "The Violent Machine," *New Internationalist*, August 2001, 24–25.

121 Ibid.

122 Jonathan Watts, "Mao Returns to Haunt and Comfort His People," *Guardian*, December 27, 2003, http://www .longmarchspace.com/ media/guardian %20unlimiter.htm (October 21, 2006).

122 *Taipei Times,* "Mao Zedong Joins the Pantheon of China's Folk Gods," September 6, 2006, http://www.taipeitimes.com/News/world/archives/2006/09/06/2003326405 (October 21, 2006).

123 *Monthly Review,* "On December 24, 2004, Maoists in China Get Three Year Prison Sentences for Leafleting," January 2005, http://www.monthlyreview.org/0105commentary.htm (October 21, 2006).

123 Joseph Kahn, "Where's Mao? Chinese Revise History Books," *New York Times,* September 1, 2006, A1.

123 Ibid.

124 Ken Gewertz, "Mao Under a Microscope," *Harvard University Gazette,* December 11, 2003, http://www.news.harvard.edu/gazette/2003/12.11/23-mao.html (October 23, 2006).

125 Mao Zedong, *Quotations from Chairman Mao Tse-tung* (Peking: Foreign Languages Press, 1976), 147, 199.

FURTHER READING & WEBSITES

BOOKS

Becker, Jasper. *Hungry Ghosts: Mao's Secret Famine.* New York: Free Press, 1996. Becker, a reporter, describes in horrifying detail how the famine during China's Great Leap Forward caused millions to starve and drove many to cannibalism and insanity.

Behnke, Alison. *China in Pictures.* Minneapolis: Twenty-First Century Books, 2003. This title in the Visual Geography Series enhances readers' knowledge of China's geography, people, history, government, economy, and cultural life.

Chen, Da. *China's Son: Growing Up in the Cultural Revolution.* New York: Delacorte Press, 2001. This is an easy-to-read account of a young Chinese boy and his intellectual family living through and being shattered by the Cultural Revolution.

Goldstein, Margaret. *V. I. Lenin.* Minneapolis: Twenty-First Century Books, 2007. This book follows the life and career of the world's first Communist dictator and founder of the Soviet Union.

Jiang, Ji-Li. *Red Scarf Girl: A Memoir of the Cultural Revolution.* New York: HarperCollins, 1997. As the title of this young adult book suggests, this is a story of Jiang Ji-Li, who wanted to be a Red Guard but was disqualified and discriminated against because her Communist family was accused of being "rightist" during the upheaval of the Cultural Revolution.

Jung Chang. *Wild Swans: Three Daughters of China.* New York: Anchor/Doubleday, 1991. In this award-winning book, Jung Chang describes the lives of three generations of Chinese women: her grandmother, her mother, and herself.

Malaspina, Ann. *The Chinese Revolution and Mao Zedong in World History.* Berkeley Heights, NJ: Enslow Publishers, 2004. Learn about Mao's life and the Chinese revolution from this book for young adults.

Spence, Jonathan. *Mao Zedong.* New York: Penguin Group, 2006. This is a brief and readable account of Mao Zedong's life written by a highly regarded China scholar.

Stewart, Whitney. *Deng Xiaoping: Leader in a Changing China.* Minneapolis: Twenty-First Century Books, 2001. This is a biography of Mao's successor.

————. *Mao Zedong.* Minneapolis: Twenty-First Century Books, 2006. Learn more about the life of Mao from this biography of the Chinese leader.

Zuehlke, Jeffrey. *Joseph Stalin.* Minneapolis: Twenty-First Century Books, 2006. This is a biography of the Soviet dictator, from whom Mao drew great inspiration.

WEBSITES

Chinese History Chart
http://sacu.org/histchart.html
This page on the Society of Anglo-Chinese Understanding website provides a quick look at Chinese history from the age of the dynasties to the Olympic Games scheduled for 2008 in Beijing.

A Country Study: China
http://lcweb2.loc.gov/frd/cs/cntoc.html
This is a study of China created by the U.S. Library of Congress Federal Research Division.

The Gate and the Square
http://www.tsquare.tv/tour/ga.html
This is an interactive website that allows the viewer to take a virtual tour of Tiananmen Square.

Nixon in China
http://www.gmu.edu/library/specialcollections/nixon_in_china.html
Nixon's visit to China is portrayed in a series of photographs on this site.

Stefan Landsberger's Chinese Propaganda Poster Pages

http://www.iisg.nl/~landsberger/

This site has numerous CCP propaganda posters, showing key people and events in Mao's China along with brief explanations of each poster.

Works of Mao Zedong by Date

http://www.marxists.org/reference/archive/mao/selected-works/date-index.htm

Many of Mao Zedong's speeches and writings from the *Selected Works of Mao Tse-Tung* are posted on this site.

INDEX

advanced Communism, 32
Agrarian Reform Law, 84–85
agricultural output, 65–67, 83–85
Anti-Comintern Pact, 42
Anti-Rightist Campaign, 61
arts and music, 81–83, 106

Becker, Jasper, 68
Beijing/Beiping, 44
big-character posters, 82
Bitter Winds: A Memoir of My Years in China's Gulag (Wu), 121
Bolshevik Party, 24
Boxer Rebellion, 14–16

capitalism, 32
Chen Hang-sen, 57
Chiang Kai-shek, 126; fights Mao's Red Army, 35–41; founds Whampoa Military Academy, 29; kidnapped by Zhang Xueliang, 41; in KMT, 30, 33; splits with CCP, 34
China. *See* People's Republic of China
Chinese Communist Party (CCP): Agrarian Reform Law, 84–85; alliance with KMT, 29–30; Central Committee, 117; First Five-Year Plan, 57–60; founds People's Republic of China, 47; Great Leap Forward (Second Five-Year Plan), 62–69; history of, 120; Hua Guofeng as chairman, 113–116; Mao becomes leader again, 77; Mao loses leadership of, 71; Mao's legacy in, 123; origins of, 27–29; power struggles in, 96–105; propaganda, 80;

reunites with KMT to fight Japan, 41–43; split with KMT, 34
Cold War, 55
Communist Manifesto, The, 26–27
Cultural Revolution, 72–77, 102, 120
Culture of Power: The Lin Biao Incident in the Cultural Revolution (Qiu Jin), 98–99

Dai Huang, 61
Dali Yang, 68–69
dazibao, 82
democracy, 16
Deng Xiaoping, 126; economic reforms of, 116–118; named vice premier, 100; removed from office in Cultural Revolution, 72; rises to leadership, 71; and Zhou Enlai's death, 103–104
détente, 94
Double Ten National Day, 17–18

Engels, Friedrich, 26–27

famine, 67–69
feudalism, 32
First Five-Year Plan, 57–60
Five Antis Campaign, 57
Five-Stage theory of history, 32
foreign affairs, 87–95

Gang of Four, 99, 103, 114–115, 118–119, 128
Great Leap Forward (Second Five-Year Plan), 62–73
Great Proletarian Cultural Revolution, 72–77
Guillermaz, Jacques, 28

He Zizhen, 36, 40, 127
Hoarfrost, Judy, 90
Hong Kong, 12
Hsien Feng, 126–127
Hua Guofeng, 103, 105, 113–114
Hunan Province, 12
Hundred Flowers Campaign, 60–61

Japan: aggression in 1930s, 42–45; invades Manchuria, 40; in World War I, 21–23
Jiang Ji-Li, 74–75
Jiang Qing: 100–102, 128; arrest and trial, 115, 118–119; and Cultural Revolution, 83, 102; Mao marries, 72; and party succession, 99–100
Jiangxi Soviet, 37
Jinggangshan Province, 34–37
Jung Chang, 85, 115

Khrushchev, Nikita, 69–70, 88
Kim Il Sung, 52–53
Kissinger, Henry, 92–93
Korean War, 52–55
Kuomintang (KMT) (Nationalist Party): alliance with CCP, 29–30; in exile on Taiwan, 56; fights Mao's Red Army, 35–41; loses position to CCP after war, 45–47; origins of, 19–20; reunites with CCP to fight Japan, 41–43; split with CCP, 34

labor camps, 121
land reform, 83–85
League of Nations, 23
Lenin, Vladimir Ilyitch, 24–25
Liang Heng, 82
Li Changyu, 56
Li Min, 81
Lin Biao, 71, 77, 80, 96–99, 128–129
Lin Liguo, 98

Li Zhisui, 83, 112–113
Little Red Book, 74, 80, 125, 128
Liu Shaoqi, 71, 72
Long March, 38–39
Lugou Bridge, 42, 43

Macao, 12
Manchus, 10–11
Mao Zedong: becomes a Marxist, 26–27; birth and early years, 11–14; death, 108–109; early writings, 25–26; early years in CCP, 27–30; embalming of, 112–113; first wife, 17; health issues, 108; Hundred Flowers Campaign, 60–61; legacy of, 120–125; at liberation of Beiping, 8; and the Long March, 38–39; memorials to, 109–112; organizes Red Army, 34–37; personal life of, 105–108; schooling, 17–18; writings, 74, 80–83
Mao Zedong's Thought, 80
Mao Zemin, 12
Mao Zetan, 12
Marco Polo Bridge, 42, 43
Marriage Reform Law, 86
Marx, Karl, 24, 27
Marxism, 26–27, 32
May Fourth Movement, 23–25
media, 74
Mo Bo, 73
Moraes, Frank, 60

Nanjing, Rape of, 44
nationalism, 16
Nationalist Party. *See* Kuomintang (KMT) (Nationalist Party)
"National Shame Day," 23
Nixon, Richard M., 92–95, 129

operas, 81–83, 106

peasant movement, 31–34
Peking National University, 23
Peng Dehuai, 71
People's Republic of China—
economics: Deng's
modernization, 116–118; First
Five-Year Plan, 57–60; Great
Leap Forward, 62–69; industrial
development, 57–60, 64–66
People's Republic of China—life in:
Cultural Revolution, 72–77, 102,
120; famine years, 67–69;
media, 74; rural life, 83–85;
women's status, 86–87
People's Republic of China—
military: conflicts with USSR, 88;
Korean War, 52–55; Vietnam
War, 88–89
People's Republic of China—
politics: CCP power struggles,
96–105; Cultural Revolution,
72–77; declared, 6–7, 47; early
years after war, 48–51; foreign
affairs, 87–95; Hundred Flowers
Campaign, 60–61; modern
border, 13; persecutes political
enemies, 56–57; split with
Soviet Union, 69–70
Ping-Pong, 89–91
primitive Communism, 32

Qing dynasty, 10–11, 14–16, 18
Qiu Jin, 98–99
*Quotations from Chairman Mao
Zedong,* 74

Red Army: formation of, 34–36; rules
for soldiers, 35
Red Guards, 72–77
Red Scarf Girl (Jiang), 74–75
rural life, 83–85
Russian Revolution, 24–25

Schram, Stuart, 28
Selected Works of Mao Tse-Tung, 80
Shanghai Communiqué, 94–95
slavery, 32
Snow, Edgar, 40, 68
Socialism, 17
Soviet Union. *See* Union of Soviet
Socialist Republics (USSR)
Spence, Jonathan, 28
spheres of influence, 15
Sun Yat-sen, 16–20, 29, 129–130
Syngman Rhee, 52–53

table tennis, 89–91
Taiwan, 12
Tang Na, 101
Tangshan earthquake, 104–105
Three Antis Campaign, 56–57
Three People's Principles, 16, 19
Tiananmen Square, 8, 73, 126
Twenty-One Demands, 21, 22
Tzu Hsi (empress dowager), 15–16,
126–127

Union of Soviet Socialist Republics
(USSR), 25; conflicts with, 88; as
model for People's Republic of
China, 49–50
United Nations, 53
United States, 89–95

Versailles Peace Treaty, 23
Vietnam War, 88–89

Wang Hongwen, 99, 114–115,
118–119
Wang Yinju, 76
Whampoa Military Academy, 29,
128
*Wild Swans: Three Daughters of
China* (Chang), 85
Wilson, Woodrow, 23
women's status, 86–87

World War I, 21–23
World War II, 45–47
Wu, Harry, 121
Wuchang rebellion, 17–18

Yang Changji, 26
Yang Kaihui, 26, 29, 36, 130
Yao Wenyuan, 99, 114–115, 118–119
Yuan Shikai, 19–21, 22, 130–131

Zhang Chunqiao, 99, 114–115, 118–119

Zhang Jingyao, 26
Zhang Xueliang, 40
Zhao Youping, 8–9
Zhongnanhai, 106
Zhou Enlai: 131; and Americans, 90, 92–93; during Cultural Revolution, 72, 77; death, 102; differences with Lin, 96; in famine years, 71; meets with Kissinger, 92–93; named prime minister, 48–49; and Soviets, 88
Zhu De, 8, 34

PHOTO ACKNOWLEDGMENTS

The images in this book are used with the permission of: © Keystone/Hulton Archive/Getty Images, pp. 1, 44, 111; AP Photo, pp. 7, 43, 79, 94; © AFP/Getty Images, pp. 9, 49, 50, 59, 70, 87, 88, 103, 114, 119; © ChinaStock, pp. 11, 20 (both), 65, 66, 73, 104, 108; © Laura Westlund/Independent Picture Service, pp. 13, 46, 54; National Archives, p. 15 (left); © Hulton-Deutsch Collection/CORBIS, p. 15 (right); © Rene Burri/Magnum Photos, pp. 18, 38; © Sean Sexton Collection/CORBIS, p. 22; Library of Congress, p. 27 (left) (LC-USZ62-16530); © Pictoral Parade/Hulton Archive/Getty Images, p. 27 (right); © Three Lions/Hulton Archive/Getty Images, p. 53 (left); © Carl Mydans/Time & Life Pictures/Getty Images, p. 53 (right); © 1994 Li Zhensheng/ChinaStock, p. 75; © 1988 Li Zhensheng/ChinaStock, p. 80; © Richard Harrington/Three Lions/Getty Images, p. 82; © Bettmann/CORBIS, pp. 91, 107, 110; © Fox Photos/Hulton Archive/Getty Images, p. 101; © China Photos/Getty Images, p. 122.

Front cover: © Bill Hauser/Independent Picture Service (main); © AFP/Getty Images (background)

AUTHOR BIOGRAPHY

Kathlyn Gay is the author of more than 120 books, some written in collaboration with family members who are scattered from coast to coast. Her books focus on social and environmental issues, culture, history, health, communication, and sports. Her writing has covered a range of age levels, from "first readers" and science booklets to young adult and adult nonfiction. Gay's work has also appeared in encyclopedias, teacher manuals, and portions of textbooks. Among her other published works are hundreds of magazine features and stories; plays; and promotional materials.